AFTER THE BABY IS BORN ...

Motherhood
YOUR First 12 Months

Deborah Insel

ACROPOLIS BOOKS LTD.
Washington, D.C.

Acknowledgements:

Many thanks to all of these people who helped in direct and personal ways to bring this book to fruition.

Pari Anvar   Ruth Guyer
Mary Beth Cody   Kathie Insel
Beverly Fein   Sherrie Lyons
Carol Gay   Sandy Mulcahy

The author wishes to express appreciation to the following who granted permission to use excerpts from their books;

From THE MARRIAGE RELATIONSHIP, edited by Salo Rosenbaum and Ian Alger, (c) 1968 by Society of Medical Psychoanalysts, Basic Books, Inc., Publishers, New York.

From IDENTITY AND THE LIFE CYCLE by Erik H. Erikson. (Psychological Issues, 1959). Copyright 1959 by International Universities Press, Inc., and Copyright (c) 1980 by W.W. Norton & Company Inc. Used by permission of the publisher.

©Copyright 1982 by Acropolis Books Ltd.

ACROPOLIS BOOKS LTD.   Printed in the United States of America by
Colortone Building, 2400 17th St., N.W.   COLORTONE PRESS, Creative Graphics Inc.
Washington, D.C. 20009   Washington, D.C. 20009

ATTENTION: Schools and Corporations

ACROPOLIS books are available at quantity discounts with bulk purchase for educational, business, or sales promotional use. For information, please write to: SPECIAL SALES DEPARTMENT, ACROPOLIS BOOKS LTD., 2400 17th ST, NW, WASHINGTON, D.C. 20009

Are there ACROPOLIS Books you want but cannot find in your local stores?

You can get any Acropolis book title in print. Simply send title and retail price, plus 50% per copy to cover mailing and handling costs for each book desired. District of Columbia residents add applicable sales tax. Enclose check or money order only, no cash please, to:
ACROPOLIS BOOKS LTD., 2400 17th ST., NW WASHINGTON, D.C. 20009

OR SEND FOR OUR COMPLETE CATALOGUE OF ACROPOLIS BOOKS.

Library of Congress Cataloging in Publication Data

Insel, Deborah, 1949-
   Motherhood, the first 12 months.

   Bibliography: p.
   Includes index.
   1. Mothers—Psychology. I. Title. II. Title:
Motherhood, the first twelve months.
HQ759.I55   1982   306.8'743   16321
ISBN 0-87491-497-3
ISBN 0-87491-498-1 (pbk.)

To my mother, Wanda Mae Silber

"Life gives unto life"
She taught me how.

CONTENTS

F O R E W O R D

There is an ancient story about a mysterious woman who each morning carries a large basket across the border into a hostile country. The basket is filled with straw. A border guard, suspicious that the woman is smuggling, inspects the basket each morning. He sifts through the straw, but each day he finds neither weapons nor contraband, so reluctantly he allows her to pass. The ritual continues day after day, month after month, much to the border guard's dismay. The mystery is solved years later after the two countries enter an interlude of peace.

The border guard, meeting the woman under more friendly circumstances, beseeches her, "Now you must tell me, what were you hiding from me, what were you smuggling across the border?" The woman responds with a faint smile, "Baskets, only baskets."

This story comes to mind when thinking of the process of becoming a parent. So much attention has been paid to the contents and so little to the container. There are books on pregnancy and birthing and how-to guides for the first year. There are automatic swings, disposable diapers, even recordings of placental sounds—parenting aids scarcely dreamed of a generation ago. There are classes for mothers who breast-feed. There are monthly mail-order guides to playing with a child in his or her first year. Birthing has become big business, parenting has become an industry, and yet the process of becoming a parent—that ancient, primal rite—has been, like the baskets in the story, almost totally overlooked.

Why this should happen is in itself an interesting question. Certainly, one explanation could be that this process is too intimate and private for the public eye. This is the principle according to which we talk the most about what is least important and talk least about things that really matter. Another explanation is that new mothers, and new fathers, are an oppressed lot who have time for neither reading nor writing. When time for such luxuries arrives, the mother and father are no longer "new" and their memories of the hard times just passed are no longer accurate. This outlook, of great survival value for the species, minimizes recent hardships, maximizes the satisfactions, and keeps attention focused on the "better days ahead." A third explanation is that there is a certain mystery in the process of becoming a parent which defies clear descriptions. There is an event which marks the outer transition, as in becoming a wife or a widow, but the inner transformation happens on its own individual time-course, in its own way. In fact parenthood, in a psychological sense, does begin long before the pregnancy and continues long after the last child leaves home. Such a process is much less conspicuous than the transition events, the landmarks such as the wedding, the birth, the death, that we can all witness and on which we expend so much energy.

Whatever the reasons for past neglect of the process, this book attempts to reverse the trend. The author includes experiences from her own emotional odyssey, reports of other women, and the descriptions of several psychologists interested in the process of development. Development, it is assumed here, is a lifelong process, and the author's major point is that becoming a parent represents one of the most difficult and most fulfilling elements of this process. For expectant parents, the descriptions of the most difficult times may seem overly grim. Parents of older children may have the same response. Curiously, new parents who have read this book (perhaps during a 3 A.M. feeding) have just the opposite response. For them, the hardships, the self-doubt, the sleeplessness, the loneliness, seem a little understated.

Certainly for the author, my wife, the process was a stormy one. For her, becoming a parent was mixed with losing a parent. Her mother died suddenly just six weeks before our first child was born. The birth itself was unusually arduous and complicated. Holding the baby in those early weeks, she developed a new sense of identification with her own mother and then a new depth of grief as she realized what she had so recently lost. Joy mingled with sorrow.

It was the turmoil of this time that led her to find out more from other women about their experiences with becoming mothers. To her surprise, motherhood was not all joy and fulfillment even for women not grieving. For many it was a stormy passage made even stormier by a belief that everyone else was problem-free. Sometime during these early months, she resolved to dispel the myth of mothering as a natural skill, both as a tribute to her own mother and as a balm to the mother within.

That was a few years ago. We have had a second child since then. Rereading this book now, I'm reminded of a time soon after our first child was born when I was talking to an older colleague about the amount of work this little creature required. The colleague, a child psychiatrist, put his hand on my shoulder and repeated what he had been told a generation earlier about parenting. "Nobody gets any medals in this business." His point, which I didn't understand for several days, is a main message of this book. There is no best way and there is no easy way through the transition of becoming a parent. Trust your feelings, share your doubts, and take note. The process is never-ending and irreversible. It preceded us as individuals and as a species. We cannot understand much of it, but we can experience it. The experiencing of that vast odyssey of emotions is what this book helps us through.

THOMAS INSEL, M.D.

Staff Psychiatrist,
National Institutes
of Mental Health

P R E F A C E

When I became a mother for the first time, I was stunned by the endless amount of work and time it took to care for a newborn. I had no idea there would be so many sleepless nights in a row, or that I would want to be so totally given over to the child. It took what I thought was a suprisingly long time to recover physically. And I agonized over feeling that I would never be a separate person again. One moment, I resented my son for what I felt was his destruction of me; the next, I was remorseful for blaming this small person I loved so deeply. I felt off-balance and mildly confused for months.

Rushing to the library for books of explanations and insights, I found there were none. Because of that, I began to feel that something was wrong with me: I could not cope as naturally as most mothers did. I muddled through as best I could, feeling insecure and inadequate—until an amazing thing happened. My friends started having babies, and they experienced many of the same traumas that I had. There was a universal quality to the challenges of transition to motherhood, and I began to notice some patterns.

We are, as modern, educated women, immensely prepared for the birth process through books and classes, hospital tours, and movies. By the time our due dates come up on the calendar we know all the signs of the beginning of labor, all the stages we will have to go through; we know what kind of atmosphere we want the child to be born into. But we know little about what to expect from the child that will soon be ours—and less about the realities of motherhood. Most of us have no idea of the tremendous emotional adjustments we will have to make. If in the past women grew up surrounded by infant cousins, siblings or friends' babies, and were thus familiar and more or less comfortable with these demanding little creatures, just the opposite has been true in our generation. Our experience has not consisted of growing up in families with sprawling age ranges and extended families, but of compact entities in which older children had little or no contact with infants. And as a grouop, we've deferred our childbearing, so that we haven't even been able to see how our friends cope with children.

There is absolutely nothing like the drastic experience of giving birth. Not only is it probably the most grueling physical task of our lives, but we are also suddenly mothers to beings who will consume—with all their needs, and with all our loving worrying—nearly all our energy for the next several months. In a very short time we have to reorient ourselves in relation to our men and in relation to our own self-concepts. Life is never the same after having a baby, and that is a huge fact to realize. No one prepared us for all this. And it can come as quite a shock.

We have probably all had the experience of listening to our mothers or other women ramble on about their delivery experiences or the trying first years of their children's lives. Or, closer to home, we have probably felt a great need in ourselves to go over and over the pregnancy and events surrounding the birth of our child. We wish we had more listeners. Giving birth and raising children is an elemental life experience that continues to shock and amaze us in its intensity for years. It is, therefore, not surprising that we enjoy sharing anecdotes, reading about it, and discussing it whenever possible. The first few weeks are dramatic, but the whole process is, in itself, profound.

In the days and weeks that follow the birth, hundreds of questions come up. "Will I ever regain my old body size?" "Should I try to get the baby on a schedule?" "Will there ever be time for just me again?" And when there are few friends who've been through it or reassuring grandmothers around to give encouragement, the questions can turn into anxieties that sap our strength even more.

Most books tend to breeze through the early postpartum months, a time when we need very specific details about our feelings and affirmation of them—the kinds of information we were used to during the pregnancy. But suddenly there is a dearth of material. Not only can it be intimidating to face all of the new emotions relatively alone, but the lack of information tends to make us feel as though we *should* be coping better and not worrying so much about the "natural, feminine role." It might be natural, but it surely isn't familiar. And it most certainly *is* overwhelming.

Aside from all the practical, day-to-day aspects of motherhood, which are hard enough to adjust to, becoming a mother is a major maturational step in the life of a woman. It involves a period of emotional transition into a new, permanently altered self. The adjustment *must* take place, and it cannot be rushed. All of these processes are underestimated, and mostly not even observed, in previous books written for mothers.

This book specifically does not deal with "how-to" advice.

(Occasionally there are references to books that are particularly helpful on a given subject.) But rather, this is a description and exploration of the many and complex facets of normal emotional growth into motherhood. It is a book about women observing and nurturing their own development as well as their children's.

I have generally followed a month-by-month sequence, partly because some of our adjusting has to be done in conjunction with the child's growth. But mostly I have done so to emphasize that emotional adjustment to motherhood takes a very long time. It is not finished at the end of the first year by any means, although we are better able to cope with our changing identities by then. Of course children and mothers develop individually, according to their own schedules, and what one mother might be experiencing during the third month, another might in the seventh, so the book should be read accordingly.

The three chapters which do not follow a time sequence concern important relationships in which there will probably be a flare-up of emotions. These chapters—on the newborn, the couple, and grandparents—follow the first chapter, because intricate developmental changes might begin to occur in those relationships during the first few weeks. Once again, though, actual awareness of these changes might not happen until later.

For the most part, I have assumed a traditional, albeit contemporary family. A few wonderful souls are experimenting with alternative family styles, and many of us are varying the traditional roles as much as practicalities will allow, but basically the men are still the main breadwinners and the mothers still hold primary responsibility for the child care in most families. The feelings that the majority of us have are what I have addressed.

In part, I hope to explain finally to myself why becoming a mother was such a chaotic experience; and I hope, too, by writing about mothering to help other new mothers. My sources include obstetrical textbooks and recent studies, and perhaps more important, mothers who answered questionnaires and voiced their experiences and emotions as they traversed that difficult first year with their children.

Being a mother, as far as I can tell, is a constantly evolving process of adapting to the needs of your child while also changing and growing as a person in your own right. These are a lot of acts to juggle, and things rarely go smoothly. But it does seem to get a little easier after a couple of years of practice. I hope this book may be of some use in easing the initial transitions that can be so overwhelming but are so necessary.

Best of luck.

DEBORAH INSEL

THE FIRST TRANSITIONS

Giving birth and becoming a mother is one of life's great events. But because it is not celebrated—for the mother—with any sort of formal ceremony, like a graduation or a marriage, the enormity of the transition is generally not recognized. For any other of life's major "passages," there is lengthy preparation—such as years of schooling—that eases us into the new role. For women, there are the nine rather short months of pregnancy when the focus, for first-time mothers, is more on what is happening in and to their bodies.

One reason becoming a mother has not been seen as a major transition is because as women, we've been brought up to believe in our inherent feminine capabilities to be mothers. Motherhood supposedly happens as normally and almost as effortlessly as menstruation. All of society reinforces the myth that women will slip into the maternal role as easily as changing into a new pair of shoes.

The emphasis on natural childbearing, too, for all its advantages, tends to reinforce the notion that mothering is a natural, spontaneous, unlearned facility endowed upon all women who conceive and labor. Of course a woman is transformed into a mother at the instant of her child's birth, but the full transition—the adjustment to motherhood—actually takes months and years. It involves not only on-the-spot learning of new skills, but also complex emotional developments.

Virtually overnight we are asked to assume a new role that is completely alien, but that is supremely important for the well-being of the child. We wouldn't have it any other way. After a few hours or days, our feelings of attachment to, and protectiveness of that child are overwhelming. We love and need the baby. And yet, the sudden change and necessary adjustments keep us in a state of disequilibrium for a long time, while the evolution to motherhood is occurring.

These weeks and months of confusion and bewilderment, experienced by all new mothers, are not generally discussed—in view of the belief that mothering is so natural. And so, at a time when we feel we most need affirmation of our emotions, we also feel that we can't talk about them. People would think us inadequate mothers.

We tend to struggle through on our own. And eventually, time and experience ease our worries and conflicts, but not without those months of restlessness that are symptomatic of the fundamental changes taking place in our psyches.

The earliest transitions take place almost without our knowledge in the first ecstatic, confusing, demanding postpartum days. We experience the end of the pregnancy and the beginning of a new theme in our lives in the midst of a fog. Some of this confusion is simply the whirlwind of enormous events that have occurred and continue to occur, such as the labor and delivery, the excitement of finally meeting the stranger we've been carrying around and the beginning of lactation. But part of the fog is also the conflicting, puzzling emotions that suddenly rush in on us, signaling the reorganization necessary to becoming a mother.

Our Bodies—The First Major Transition Is A Physical One

Even though giving birth is the working out of a natural process, it is, nevertheless, a physically traumatic, exhausting experience. There are no other normal circumstances under which the body goes through such upheaval and change in such a short period. As a maternity nursing textbook puts it, "Specific anatomic and physiologic changes ... occur abruptly and are sizable. They involve profound diminution in circulating blood volume, a weight loss, displacement of internal organs, etc. It is truly marvelous that the new parturient [the newly delivered mother] copes so adequately and that she complains so little."[1]

If we complain so little it's because we are in such a daze at all that is suddenly happening to us physically. The nine months of gradual bodily change come to a crashing halt with delivery, and then there are a variety of discomforts and strange, unexpected physical developments. All at once, within several hours of finishing labor, we are trying to regain control of bladder and bowels, fumbling with belts and pads to cope with the uterine discharge, even though we still can't see over our bellies to our genitals, and attempting to find comfortable positions for our sore bottoms. Having just emerged from the ordeal of labor, desiring merely to rest and recuperate, these new problems can be dizzying. Psychologically, it is defeating to see that our abdomens are anything but flat. We still look seven months pregnant.

A widespread misconception has it that "true" women give birth without so much as a whimper and return to work, baby strapped to their backs, all in the same day. If not to that extreme, certainly most parents expect that the mother will be restored to normal within a couple of weeks and can resume her usual activities almost immediately after that. This simply isn't true. Obstetricians don't consider us "anatomically normal" again for at least six weeks, the length of time it takes before the reproductive tract returns to its pre-pregnancy size and position; and most women feel that it takes much longer to regain their original body shape and usual energy levels. Physical regeneration is a slow, steady process undertaken after extreme stress. That's what the fragile postpartum period is.

Consider all that is happening. The uterus begins immediately to contract and fall, so that at the end of labor, its upper edge is below the navel. Ten days later it is already completely back in the pelvic cavity, which means that it can't be felt above the pubic bone. This rapid decrease in the size of an organ (to one-twentieth its size at the onset of labor) is seen in no other circumstances except illness.[2]

This involutionary process is rapid and dramatic, and is marked by sometimes severe afterpains of the uterus contracting, especially when the baby nurses. The uterus is shedding excess material that made up some of its bulk in the lochia, or discharge, through the vagina. The discharge, reddish in color, is quite heavy at first, requiring the use of hospital-sized sanitary napkins and frequent changes. It tapers off as it changes to yellowish color. Sometimes there are clots and tissue in the discharge. And it can last as long as a couple of months.

The cervix, on the other hand, instead of sloughing material, is adding new tissue, healing any tears that might have occurred and slowly closing the opening to the uterus. After ten days it is usually closed again, though it takes several weeks to completely return to normal.

The vagina requires several weeks to recover. It remains stretched and smooth-walled for about three weeks. But as it gradually diminishes in size the normal folds and ridges return, though it rarely returns completely to its pre-pregnancy condition.[3] Some women report more sensitivity in their vaginas after having had a baby, some report a different shape, but no loss of sensitivity; and there is probably quite a range of experience.

Usually urination occurs without too much difficulty even though the ureter has been traumatized and swollen during the birth, and the bladder has been compressed for months. These structures take about four weeks to reposition and heal. Some women do have urination problems though, and bladder infections can develop as a result.

The bowel is sluggish generally, being suddenly awash in much more space and lacking tone. The abdominal muscles, because of the extreme extension of pregnancy, have little strength with which to push, and with the soreness down below, we're not sure we want to anyway. Constipation plagues most mothers for a few days. Many women describe as one of the worst early problems the desire to defecate and the fear of it as well. Hemorrhoids are common.

Between the third and the fifth day, the body begins to reduce its excess blood volume by discharging waste products and water through the urine and perspiration. Normally, such rapid and extensive excretion would cause exhaustion and extreme weakness.[4]

There can be a loss of ten to twenty pounds in one week which, in any other situation, "would throw a person into shock."[5] And the internal organs all have to reposition abruptly and adjust to the new size and shape of the mother. Under other circumstances, this would be an "excruciatingly painful experience."[6]

The breasts remain in their pregnant state for about two days after the birth, then begin lactating. They become larger, firmer, more tender and can become engorged with milk. The nursing baby, of course, helps relieve the tightness, but nursing is not really established, with a good balance between adequate supply without engorgement, for a few weeks.

I dwell on these inelegant aspects of physical recovery because as well prepared as we are for what will happen to our bodies in labor, most women know nothing about what transpires afterward. They wonder why they don't "bounce back," why they fatigue easily or feel faint. All this sudden physical change and regeneration requires vast amounts of energy.

> *"All of a sudden the messiness of the birth, the continual bleeding afterwards, the dripping of my breasts, not having good control of my Kegel muscles [floor of the pelvis muscles] just disgusted me. Here was a biologist who, in fact, had been fascinated with all the biological aspects of the process, and I did not even look at the placenta."*

> *"I was exhausted. I didn't expect to be as weak as I was for so many days. I just wanted to sleep, sleep, sleep, and I couldn't. Even though I had no tears or an episiotomy, my bottom was very sore."*

> *"I couldn't have imagined wearing two sanitary pads and an ice pack all at once. Going to the bathroom and changing all that stuff in those first weak days was a major endeavor."*

> *"Several friends hurt my feelings by remarking that I still looked pregnant. Though I knew their observations were accurate, I felt like a person who'd just lost twenty pounds on a weight-watchers diet to whom someone says, 'Yes, but you still look awfully chunky.' "*

"For the first eighteen hours after the birth I was more exhausted than I'd ever been in my life. I couldn't even walk to the bathroom by myself without becoming faint. When I first looked in the mirror, I looked like someone had just punched me in both eyes. I was astounded by how weak I could be."

Emotions

The purpose of obstetrics is to deliver the "products of conception" and to assure that the woman is returned to her normal physical state in the course of due time. Doctors, in general, do not have time to notice the complex of emotions swirling in their patients. Unless something goes wrong in the postpartum period, the obstetrician considers the job finished and feels that "nature can take its course" from there on. Yet we are transformed from bodies heavy with pregnancy to mothers laden with weak bodies and strange, shadowy new emotions.

"Throughout the pregnancy I concentrated on the astounding changes that were happening to my body. Of course, I loved feeling the baby kick, but it was such an anonymous being, and I had no idea what actually having a baby meant—that a lot of the time, in retrospect, it seems like I was more concerned about me than about the baby. That was true in labor and right afterward, too. It was all happening to me, and it was a while before I could devote attention to the baby, and realize that he had been through it too."

The beginning of labor is a usually joyous social time between our men and ourselves. Finally the long-awaited event is going to happen after we had begun to give up hope that it ever would. We breathe together and synchronize our emotions. We share and divide whatever frustrations there might be about the progress of labor or hospital practices, and labor starts exuberantly. But then as the contractions become more intense, we begin to be less sociable. We spiral down into ourselves, almost hypnotically, to concentrate. Sounds in the room seem far away, time passing has no meaning, suggestions made about our position or breathing seem intrusive. We are deep withing ourselves, hoarding strength, almost completely unaware of our men, the babies or the staff. Our total attention is riveted on the irreversible events occurring in our bodies.

We surface to hear the baby cry and to clasp hands with our man. There's the first meeting with the baby and everyone's comments and congratulations, then the afterbirth to force out. We are glad that the ordeal is over and the baby is healthy, but we remain in something of a daze for awhile. Even if we've been unmedicated throughout the labor and birth, there is a dreamlike quality to the experience that lingers for hours, even days after delivery. Women who have given birth in the familiar surroundings of home and friends, as well as women who deliver in hospitals describe this same postpartum haze. We're able to function fairly rationally, but there is an unreal quality to things.

The first couple of postpartum weeks have been described by one author in terms of two phases. The first aspect, called the "taking-in phase," is said to last two or three days while we slowly open out again from the profoundly in-drawn, defensive position reached in the hardest parts of labor.[7] We begin to relive the delivery by asking questions about specific details and by describing our impressions of it. By piecing together this total picture, we are trying to integrate it fully with reality and are attempting to realize that the pregnancy and birth are truly over, that the baby is now a separate individual. That kind of awareness does not come quickly, especially given that our sensory receptors were partly sealed over in reaction to pain.

In this "taking-in phase" we are passive and dependent, trying to do what we are told and gratefully accepting what is given to us. We initiate little or no action since even simple decisions, as well as slight physical activity, fatigue us. Our needs are more in relation to ourselves than to our babies. It is a restorative time in which sleep and food are very important.[8] And we only slowly begin to unfold to the world again.

At the end of about three days, the dependence gives way to a desire to take control and assume our new responsibilities. The fog lifts, and we see all around us things that need to be done. We feel an urgency to control bodily functions, thinking that if we can't do that we can't really do anything else. We want to get the nursing off to a good start now that the milk has just come in. And we feel as though we should walk and sit more normally so we can accomplish what is needed. This has been labeled the "taking-hold phase."[9] We "move from the resting and recuperating phase, which was determined by the events of the immediate past, to embracing a commitment to the immediate present."[10]

Success at the first mothering tasks is especially important to us as a sign of independence and control. And suddenly we begin to be flooded with brand-new feelings about this little life that we had not expected. We want to do a good job for the sake of the baby: it's so unprotected, and we're all it's got!

Now the baby's needs are uppermost. We have lots of questions and need reassurance concerning our handling and care of the baby, particularly about feeding and crying. There are also questions about bathing, care of the navel, circumcision, sleeping and weight gain, rashes, and taking the baby out. It's all new, and we begin to feel the immense responsibility of it. We want to grab the reins, and feel mature and loving and efficient. Now is the chance to demonstrate our native maternal abilities—our own expectations and society's expectations demand it of us. But we are constantly brought down to reality by inexperience, feelings of awkwardness, and frequent inability to soothe the baby.

"When we first came home from the hospital, the baby fell into a deep sleep probably because of the rhythmic sound and motion of the car. Any amount of jostling and rubbing his cheeks wouldn't disturb him. We were horrified, convinced he had died. We just didn't know that cars put babies to sleep."

Frustrations or failures may cause us to worry and be hypercritical about our abilities. In these intense few days we are particularly vulnerable to anyone's off-hand comments and to the baby's response to us. We have frequent and rapid mood swings because of heightened sensitivities.

"I was unable to concentrate on anything but the baby, but also I was hypersensitive. It would take nothing to set me off on huge crying jags. I felt I had no control of my emotions. People would be kind to me, and that would make me cry."

Cesarean Sections

About one of every five births in the United States is by cesarean section. Even though it is a relatively common occurrence, and most women have told themselves during the pregnancy that it is a possibility, they probably did not truly consider becoming one of the statistics.

For a first-time mother a cesarean is usually a shock and a disappointment. After hours of labor, pain, and frustration, surgery is called for. It seems a new terror and a sudden dashing of hopes for a quiet, serene birth experience.

But at the same time, it is a relief. If a cesarean is recommended, chances are the labor has gone on too long or has proceeded abnormally. The woman is exhausted and simply wants a cessation of the contractions. Further, she is promised that she can be holding the baby within a sort time. Disappointments about not having a perfect birth are put aside under the circumstances.

> *"After forty hours of labor that came and went but generally got more and more intense, I wasn't the least bit upset at having a C-section. At that point, in fact, I would have preferred to die rather than go on with the labor, I was so wiped out. To be able to have it all over and the baby delivered seemed impossibly beautiful. And I had been a fanatical natural birther."*

> *"I had a cesarean after twenty-four hours of labor. I was too tired to push, so at the time, I was glad to have that option. But I was sad later at not actually feeling the baby slither out. I sometimes feel like I've missed the true birth experience that my friends talk about. And I'm going to try to have a normal delivery with my next baby."*

Some mothers' feelings go further than disappointment. Some blame themselves or feel that they've failed for not giving birth "normally." There might be an element of this feeling in all cesarean section mothers. Such feelings are real and legitimate, of course, but unnecessary.

The reason for a higher incidence of surgical deliveries now is generally the more sensitive monitoring of the fetus. When the fetus registers any distress, in terms of slower or irregular heart rates, the doctors think of surgery. We are not weaker or less competent women for not delivering vaginally. We are acquiescing to the sophistication of modern medicine that is ultimately giving us fewer birth-damaged babies.

Perhaps our particular baby might not have suffered. Perhaps we eventually would have pushed the baby out. Perhaps the labor would have picked up and progressed normally, and perhaps a vaginal birth would have been beautiful and fulfilling. Perhaps. But what is the use of blaming ourself for what the body did or did not do? After all, unlike the mothers who had vaginal births, many of those with cesareans heroically put up with frustrating, ultimately futile labor *and* had major surgery on top of it. Far from being failures, these mothers are to be commended for their bravery and stamina!

After the initial trauma of the birth, there is a longer, slower recovery, of course. As hard as it is for any new mother to integrate the birth process into her experience, and take charge of herself and the baby from then on, it is twice as hard for cesarean patients, since it is days and weeks before they can even sit up or walk normally. In the hospital, they are linked to tubes and under medication for several days. Just finding a comfortable position in which to cuddle the baby is difficult. When other mothers are cheerfully going to classes down the hall to learn how to bathe or burp their babies, they are struggling to inch their legs out of bed, shuffling to the bathroom, and trying to brush their teeth without spitting and therefore, contracting sore, sutured abdominal muscles.

A cesarean section is major surgery, and under any other circumstances—an appendectomy, say—the patient would be allowed weeks to recover and be pampered with care and concern. Too often, however, because birth is a normal procedure and because the baby is so needy, the cesarean mother's physical recovery is subsumed in the other new details of life. We are required to be up and about as quickly as possible for the round-the-clock feedings, diaperings, and soothings. And we *want* to be able to charge forward with mothering despite the surgery. But we have to stay longer in the hospital, we are told not to drive and to be careful with stairs; the wound is often painful and sore for several weeks, and we are exhausted from the combination of the long labor and surgery. In short, we feel as if we are stumbling in the first few weeks, trying to do more than we can, and held back by our requisite recovery time.

"I believed all the philosophy about bonding and how the mother and baby had to be together in the first hours and days. So I tried to do everything as if I hadn't had a C-section. I insisted on rooming-in so I could have him with me all the time. But I couldn't really care for him. He'd cry in the bassinette next to my bed, and I'd raise my bed, struggle and strain in pain to reach to pick him up, and I couldn't.

"So I'd call the nurse to hand him to me or to change his diaper. Then the nurses got angry and said I shouldn't have rooming-in if I couldn't manage it. So I got angry and insisted on leaving the hospital after only two days. Home was a little better, but then the meals needed to be fixed, the laundry done, the baby cared for. My husband was shortly as wiped out as I was. He was taking care of the baby and an invalid, . too. It was a very tough time. I should have just taken care of myself a little better from the beginning so I could have been stronger faster."

The Baby

Soon, self-absorption gives way to awe. Studies have shown that new mothers have a very orderly, predictable, "species-specific" pattern of exploratory behavior when they are first given their babies. It is a sort of wonder-struck claiming process that begins with fingertip touches of the child's extremities, and within a few minutes involves massaging or encompassing the baby's body with our hands.[11] We usually cuddle our babies to our left sides, closest to our hearts.[12] And it is important to us to establish eye contact with the baby as if to recognize each other's mutual existences.[13]

Mothers who are permitted to go through this intimate, never-to-be-repeated process within a few hours of birth, and who are allowed abundant time with their newborns, are found to be more quickly attached and exhibit stronger positive feelings toward their children months later.[14] Researchers note the similarities between this seemingly sensitive time for human mothers and corresponding "critical periods" for animal mothers. Many animals, for instance, won't accept their own babies after a certain time if they have been separated at birth.

This research also describes one more dimension of the postpartum whirlwind. We have a nearly instinctual need for our infants, as soon after the delivery as possible. Partly, it is curiosity finally to see what we've only fantasized about for so long. But it is also an early drive to begin to mother and love the child. We want to cuddle it, to give it the security of our arms and breasts, to reassure it that this life outside the womb can be comfortable, too. The earliest ties of affection are established then, when both we and the baby are at our weakest physically.

Some mothers are surprised at not feeling a wellspring of love right from the first moment. For them the love grows slowly, as in other relationships. Particularly around the third month, when responsive eye contact and smiles begin to come from the baby, these mothers fall in love, suddenly feeling the baby is a "person."

Other mothers feel awash in a euphoric love almost immediately, and that feeling continues and matures. But for either kind of mother, a special relationship with the child develops quickly—a kind of relationship previously unknown to us, and certainly one we never knew we were capable of fulfilling. It is simply that we begin to give totally and selflessly to another person, the baby.

We are, after all, supplying everything for this new individual, from food to changes of position to warmth. Our needs take second place behind those of the child, and we don't regret that or expect any return. A sense of responsibility has nothing whatever to do with our motivations to make the child as happy as we possibly can. This desire derives solely from the budding of a brand-new emotion—maternal love.

An overpowering sense of protectiveness sets our nerves on end when the baby cries and sends us to the side of the crib to check for the fourth time in two hours that the baby is still breathing. Without second thought, we know we would sacrifice anything for the well-being of this child. We've never seen such a cute baby, and we feel sorry for all the other new parents who weren't lucky enough to get quite such a marvelous newborn.

Our generation has been privileged. Many of us have been given a great deal by way of material things, education, the opportunity to travel. We have worked at careers for our own advancement and pleasure. Rarely, if ever, have we unselfishly devoted ourselves to anyone else's comfort or needs. If we did, we expected a reward. The altruism of motherhood is new for us, and yet we give wholeheartedly in the first weeks and hardly wish it to be any other way.

> "I think we are genetically programmed to respond to a newborn's crying. It just drove me bananas. I couldn't stand to hear it, and it made me a total rag emotionally. What would happen is she would cry, I would take care of her, and then I would cry and Michael would take care of me."

> "I was delighted to see my baby alive and separate from me, but I was also worried to death whether or not he was going to make it to the next day."

> "Not everyone is immediately elated about the baby. I wasn't. I only felt terribly weak and in pain as I thought, 'I'll never do this again!' I was also disappointed that I didn't feel elated. I had looked forward to that as a real high for my husband and me, and I only felt exhausted with almost no concern for the baby. It had all seemed like a terrible ordeal."

"Britte was very alert when she was born. Mostly, I was aware of her big size, good state of health, and her sex. I had hoped for a boy. I wasn't in the least disappointed in her sex, but I think you react different-ly to male babies than female babies, and I felt ex-tremely disoriented. I needed to sleep so badly, wanted to have Britte with me every minute, and also thought I could do both. So I gave up my sleep and watched, cuddled, and suckled her as much as possible. I was emotionally calm and fulfilled."

Breast-feeding

Lactation and breast-feeding are in a way the physiological fulfill-ment of maternal love. Just as we are beginning to accept the little creature as our own and beginning to cope with something outside of ourselves (around the third day), the milk comes in. Suddenly there is a very tangible way to express love and keep the baby close. While the baby is at the breast there is lots of time to gaze at and admire it. We gather every nuance in its expressions and begin to make inferences about its personality just by the way it nurses. The softness and warmth of the baby's body, its lightness and ap-parent fragility, its tentative open-mouthed gropings at the breast all endear it to us with a gripping power that is startling.

The pleasure, though, is often mixed with anxieties and uncertainties. Having only begun to recover from one major physical process, we begin a new, equally unfamiliar one. It is not unusual to feel very vulnerable and insecure. Instinct can go a long way to help us over this hurdle, and if we just do what feels right and hospital procedures allow us to, then most likely the nursing can get started fairly well. However, few of us feel very confident about our maternal intuitions this early in the game.

If we have read any books on breast-feeding beforehand, we

might be overloaded with data—on how many minutes to let the baby suck on each breast, remedies for sore nipples, advice on demand-versus-schedule feeding. Or worse, we might fear some latent psychological stress will surface to inhibit the "let-down reflex." As with the labor, we probably know a great deal about breast-feeding—except whether we'll be able to do it. Since this is the first major motherly chore, we are especially anxious for things to go well.

> "I had thought that having my mother around
> after the birth would disturb the breast-feeding by add-
> ing stress, so I forbade her to come until I had been
> home for a week, thinking the breast-feeding would be
> established by then. I was wrong on both counts.
> There were so many other stresses I hadn't figured on,
> and having her there would have only made things
> easier. The breast-feeding was by no means established
> in a week's time. All did go well eventually though."

There are several good, detailed books about breast-feeding that answer the multitude of questions that arise, not only at first, but throughout the months before weaning. (*Nursing Your Baby* by Karen Pryor is especially helpful.) Every mother has to find a way that suits her best, because the nursing relationship is individual.

There is no reason to feel inadequate if you find yourself reading and re-reading the same books, and the same sections, again and again, or calling doctors or friends. We need to do anything that will ease the strangeness and reassure us. This is a learning-by-doing experience, and there is a lot at stake for both the baby and mother. There is no need to feel ashamed of inexperience or awkwardness. Things usually work out surprisingly well in time. It's just that there is a great deal to learn all at once, not only about the lactation process in ourselves, but also about the baby's responses to us.

"I had my husband get one book on nursing out of the library for me during the first couple of days at home. It was the same one I'd read months before, but now everything made sense. I wanted details, day-by-day descriptions, because every day something new seemed to come up."

The fear may grip us that our milk is not good or plentiful enough to support the life of a child. After all, we never see how much the baby actually gets; the milk, when we see it drip, looks thin and blue. And besides, don't human beings need vitamins and iron and lots of other things besides milk to grow and flourish? It's intimidating and ghastly to think how much babies depend on us. We fret over the baby's weight—a loss means we're incapable and cruel, a gain is a source of enormous pride and indicates that we're actually doing something right in spite of ourselves.

"Cassandra was not very interested in sucking. She was lazy and yet hungry, so she cried at the breast, and that was terrible. I was worried that she wasn't getting enough for months as she was so small and gained slowly.

"I had a lot more ego involved than I realized. When she didn't gain I felt that somehow I had been mistreating or abusing her. Sometimes it freaked me out to think she got her total nutritional intake just from me. What a responsibility! Her life was in my hands in more ways than one. Yet I was determined to keep it up."

It is said that it takes two or three weeks to learn how to nurse and several months to become an expert.[15] We are learning a new skill in which we have a big emotional investment, and nature doesn't make it any easier. Even after the milk comes in, there is not a consistent supply that perfectly suits the baby's needs. Some days there's too much, other days there's not enough. After all, the body is learning how to do this for the first time, too. The supply does become regular eventually, but only after a couple of months. There will be some days when the breasts are engorged and leaking, when the baby sleeps a lot and seems to be on a four-hour schedule. Then there will be other days when the baby screams to be fed every two hours and our nipples are so sore we wince and push back tears as we nurse. The body's needs and the baby's needs take time to get synchronized. And if you are clock-watching, as you probably are, trying to detect a pattern in the chaos, and wishing for a pattern, things get even worse. All the discrepancies and differences day-to-day, hour-to-hour, become very clear. One of the hardest parts of breast-feeding in the first few weeks is the worrying about it.

> *"One afternoon Tom came home and I was like an apparition out of the La Leche League handbook. I had a hot hard lump in one breast and was sure I was developing mastitis. I'd heard that you have to stop breastfeeding if you get that, which now I know is not true. But anyway, I had my breastfeeding book in one hand, a hot compress for the lump in the other, a can of beer set nearby (even though I don't like beer), and I was trying to urge the baby to nurse. 'It says you've got to get the milk flowing,' I shrieked, at my wit's end."*

Another difficulty for the first few months is being "on call" around the clock every day. Sleep is what we need to recuperate and to have a good milk supply, and sleep is precisely what it is impossible to get enough of. If the baby wakes up every two or three hours to be fed and it takes a minimum of a half an hour to feed and put the baby to sleep again, that leaves an hour and a half or so for rest between feedings. Constantly interrupted sleep is a fact for weeks.

"Sleep when the baby sleeps," is the advice everyone gives, but you don't always feel sleepy then, and when you do demand sleep, the baby may be wide-eyed and hungry. Physical and spiritual exhaustion may set in—nothing in the world seems right or good. It is a depression born of pure fatigue, and usually cured by a few hours of uninterrupted, sound sleep.

The myriad of small problems with breast-feeding in the early weeks loom large bacuse of this weakened condition, and unfamiliarity with it all. To worry over each and every one is absolutely normal; to require lots of reassurance is to be expected.

On the other side of the scale are the feelings of intimacy, intensity, and well-being when things are going well with the "nursing couple." During feeding times, generally both mother and baby can relax together and share the goodness of being physically close. There is a feeling that we are giving to the baby in our own unique way, and the concentration with which the baby usually eats is reward enough.

Bottle-feeding

Of course not all mothers breast-feed. There are some good reasons not to: if you do not enjoy it, for instance, or if you are returning to work and feel that breast-feeding would be too difficult. Nevertheless, whether feeding by breast or bottle, mealtimes can be a very intimate time of sharing.

One obvious advantage to bottle-feeding is that the father can also share in this intimacy with the baby. At a time when the child is relatively unresponsive and seemingly unconnected to us, new parents may feel overwhelmed with all the details, and it is refreshing to have a peaceful time to connect with the baby, to watch it gobble down your love as you hold and lovingly give to it. That the father can have this experience and also relieve the mother so she can rest is very helpful.

There are problems with bottle-feeding, too—the baby screaming while the formula warms or having to run out for formula in the middle of the night when you thought there was an extra can on the shelf—situations that cause anxiety and tears. Or, if the formula makes the baby colicky, if the nipples are not right, if the baby wants more or less than the doctor recommends, we worry and lose sleep. Feeding is so basic—it *has* to go right.

And eventually, it does go right, the baby gains weight, is rosy, and we feel proud.

Mother and Father

For the mother and father, the first weeks are generally a time of closeness and intimacy. Strains in the relationship that might have been apparent before the birth or that will surely follow in the months to come, for the moment are submerged. The couple feels very much in love; this love is born of sharing an extremely powerful experience that is particular to them. That was no one else's delivery; and this is no one else's baby.

> *"The first month I felt totally in love with Michael. I had never felt closer. I also felt very depedent, but not in a bad way."*

> *"Our catch-phrase describing that first week or so was 'exhausted but euphoric.' We both felt very sentimental and all but overwhelmed by the intensity of the love we felt for the baby and for each other. We'd get tears in our eyes over the smallest things—just saying the word 'family,' hearing the words to a song about children, or Bill's recalling how helpless and weak I was after the birth."*

There might have been elements of crisis at the worst

moments of the labor, and there were also the tender moments when the couple was working together to hasten the process. Both the anxiety and the mutuality are remembered and cherished as symbols of unity. There is also immense relief that it's over and that all went well. There is gratitude to each other for the part each played.

The baby, of course, is in itself a source of wonder and sharing. Comparing physical features is a lighthearted way that parents usually get acquainted with their offspring. The more serious side consists of remarks of astonishment and pride that they could have created such a perfect little individual.

The father often finds himself endowed with unusual strength and stamina, able to work his regular hours, plus cook meals, do the extra laundry, and still have time and energy to sit and enjoy his new family. To him fall the supportive chores of taking care of the mother while she cares for the child. And in these days of euphoria and stress, that is how he expresses his love.

> *"I was really impressed by how patient and supportive he was, even when I was snappy or distracted. He constantly validated my feelings and seemed to know exactly what I needed to hear. I felt bad that he was doing everything—making meals, doing dishes, running errands, waiting on me, and caring for the baby a lot. And I worried about him becoming exhausted, too."*

The mother, meanwhile, is drawn to her man by her own dependence. His gentle caring and reassurance in all the vicissitudes of the first couple of weeks are the necessary antidote to the insecurities she is feeling. They share the pleasures and problems in the glow of their newly rediscovered love. It is the time about which people often say, "the baby will bring them together." And at least for now, it does accomplish that.

Blues

It is hardly surprising with all that is happening externally, and unusual hormonal fluctuations occurring internally, that some of us experience a period of blues or depression beginning a few days after the birth. This reaction is as individual as any other, from a few hours of crying to indifference and despair to, in the extreme, psychosis. Except for psychosis, these reactions are considered normal under the stressful circumstances of the postpartum period.

Most women find it essential to talk about these feelings of depression and usually feel better afterward if the listener has been sympathetic and accepting. Other women struggle through, ashamed that they should be courting such feelings at what is supposed to be a joyous time. It is important to realize that whatever feelings we're having after the birth are significant and necessary, for whatever reason.

There are many theories about why postpartum depression occurs. It may be due to endocrine imbalances, or fatigue and extreme stress, or to social factors, such as attention suddenly shifting from the pregnant woman to her newborn. The problem has not been studied extensively, because it is considered a normal state and generally clears up by itself. Unfortunately, the suffering of the women who have such depressions for a long time is not often taken into account.

There are few, if any good general books on postpartum depressions. *Our Bodies, Ourselves* does contain an insightful discussion of the depth and difficulties of these feelings but the concentration is on the farther extreme of the depression.

Other Considerations

Most of us are mature, independent women by the time we have our first babies these days, and are used to taking care of ourselves physically and emotionally. Generally, we feel in control of most situations and confident of our abilities. If the pregnancy was planned and desired, we have prepared ourselves for the upcoming event and have looked forward to it. Wisely, we counseled ourselves that there would be big changes after the baby was born, but in trying to imagine exactly what they would be, the picture was a bit murky.

After the baby comes, the situation seems to zoom out of control for a while—weeks, actually. Taking care of ourselves physically is time-consuming. We may be very dependent, even for the basics of meals, clean clothes, and sleep. For some of us this enforced dependence is hard to accept. We may feel frazzled in the grip of powerful new emotions—and not understand where they are taking us.

The ultimate responsibility for the baby comes to us—the buck stops here. Yet, we protest that we do not know enough, we have no experience. There is nothing to do but begin to learn quickly, hour by hour. And all of this happens against a backdrop of exhaustion and physical depletion.

Becoming a mother has been termed a "maturational crisis,"[16] similar to menstruation or menopause, when specific physiologic and endocrine changes together with emotional changes produce a developmental, or life-altering step. As in a musical composition, it is a stormy passage between two related, but differing themes.

> *"I definitely did not think I experienced postpartum depression, just postpartum: you don't know anything. Just when you are starting to recover from the sheer exhaustion of the birth, you have to deal with your milk coming in, trying to nurse the baby. I didn't even know how to put on a diaper, and I had total responsibility for this wonderful, demanding, totally helpless creature."*

"I had a good birth, a wonderfully sensitive and supportive spouse, excellent support from midwives, friends, and relatives who came and helped, and yet I was totally overwhelmed! In the middle of the first week when I knew Michael would be going back to school the following week, I still felt terribly weak and I was terrified that I couldn't manage. I remember crying and crying because I didn't know how I was going to be able to feed myself, or because I would just be dying to take a nap and there would be no one to look after the baby."

Suggested Reading:

The Mother Person, by Virginia Barber and Merrill Skaggs

The Mother's Book, by Ronnie Friedland and Carol Kort

Mother's Almanac, by Marguerite Kelly and Elia Parsons

Nursing Your Baby, by Karen Pryor

Having a Cesarean Baby, by Richard Hausknecht and Joan Rattner

THE NEWBORN

For the first several weeks, our world is the baby. We can do nothing more than look after the child and take care of the bare essentials for ourselves, with the former consuming most of our time. All of our emotions toward the baby are heightened, as in any intense relationship. Passing smiles or surprised expressions completely win us over, while incessant crying for two hours in the middle of the night can leave us frustrated and enraged at this apparent rejection of our attempts to soothe, especially when we might be insecure about our mothering abilities.

Preoccupied with the desire to be always with the baby, a new mother can hardly think of anything but getting back when she is away for a short period. We don't like to share the baby's attention; we are sure that no one else can care for the child as well as we can, not even the father. Highly empathetic, we try to see everything from the infant's point of view and to anticipate all its desires and needs.

In spite of all the work this devotion entails, it is a surprise to find that we enjoy the baby much of the time and that we feel so deeply about it. This is probably, above anything else, the most startling realization of all.

> *"I never expected caring for a child to be so rewarding. I think, beforehand, I perceived it to be more of a 'natural duty.' I didn't know I would really love this person. I truly feel bonded to her. To realize that even after knowing her such a short time, she would leave a huge space in our lives if she were gone is profoundly awesome to us."*

> *"I'm surprised that I am enjoying the baby so much. I never knew a newborn could be such fun. Sometimes I feel like I'm playing dolls with the most special doll of all."*

> *"I was so nervous at first with Brendan, so anxious to do everything just right that it took me a while to realize that I was falling in love with him, and that I could enjoy that feeling. I just didn't know that parents do what they do out of such a profound, spontaneous love. When the second baby came along, he got the benefit of my uncomplicated love right from the start, because I already knew what it was all about."*

Endless worrying is one form that our caring takes in these early weeks. Inexperienced, we have no idea what is normal or what we should do in any of the daily crises that plague us. The baby is a mysterious stranger who is equipped with a compelling language, cries, that no one can ignore.

It takes a certain amount of time simply to understand what newborns are like, and an even longer period of time to figure out how to deal with one's own baby in the most comfortable way for everyone concerned. We are obliged to recognize the baby's individuality and to attempt to mesh that with our own lives, while at the same time contending with all the practical realities of its daily care. Taken altogether, it is a complicated, exciting, demanding, often frustrating time.

Attachments and Expectations

Most women are startled at the intensity of what they feel for their babies. We do not all describe it as love right away, but we do seem to agree on its power. The baby and its needs block out all other concerns for the time being; we feel totally given over to the child, and we want it to be that way.

Though the baby was for so long just an anonymous being about whom we fantasized but knew nothing concrete, now the baby is real and suddenly very special. We spend literally hours gazing at and studying the child's features, smiling when the baby smiles and trying to understand the baby's moods. We think there has never before been such a remarkable child. If there are facial rashes or bruises or hair that sticks up absurdly, we are hardly aware that to others those things seem prominent. We see beneath to the beauty and perfection. (Of course, at times all of us obsess about the tiniest imperfections, but even then we are gripped by a deep sense of awe.)

The baby has a huge range of endearing expressions that indicate, we feel, some facet of its personality. If he eats greedily, we call him robust and healthy; if she is more of a taster, we call her dainty. Whatever the baby is like, we are glad and are insulted if anyone so much as suggests that it's a shame that the baby is not a little more one way or the other. What do they really know about the baby, we think, they simply aren't seeing very clearly.

Mothers soon discover that they are often the only ones who recognize and appreciate all the beauty and complexity of their babies. It comes as a frequent disappointment to us to have our child's range of behaviors and abilities, which seem so marvelous to us, go essentially unnoticed by the rest of the world. But all of this is a measure of how completely wrapped up in the child we are. No mother ever dreams beforehand that she will be so unobjectively infatuated and so quickly attached.

> *"I look back at his baby pictures now and think, 'Boy, what a funny-looking creature, covered with bumps and with worried eyebrows.' At the time I had never seen such a beautiful baby. Beautiful wasn't even a powerful enough word. Maybe . . . transcendent."*

> *"My in-laws came to see the new grandson when he was three weeks old. At one point my father-in-law remarked, 'Babies at this age are just vegetables with a few reflexes.' I was immediately incensed. It was obvious to my eyes that his grandson was far more complex and charming than that."*

Studies have shown that our babies, too, begin to single us out as special people relatively soon. For example, two-week-old babies look more at their mothers' faces than at strangers.[1] If the mother wears a white mask while feeding the baby, the baby becomes distressed and eats poorly.[2] Babies recognize and prefer their mother's voices to other voices at this stage;[3] and at six-to-ten days old, they selectively turn toward the mother's smell.[4] It seem obvious that by body contact, especially, our babies would know us, too. It is gratifying to know that the admiration is going both ways even so early on.

This special sensitivity to the baby, and the baby's to us, serves to make things both easier and more frustrating in the early weeks. Since we are so exquisitely aware of the baby, we can sometimes pinpoint what is needed to do the job right away. This ability was shown in a hospital study when newborns were brought in to their mothers over a several-day period. Even that soon, the mothers would vary their greetings and handling of the baby depending on how the baby was acting on arrival in the room.[5] They matched their behavior to the babies' cues, and this happened unconsciously and automatically. Visitors, we find, tend to hand the baby back as soon as it starts to fuss, saying, "Here, you know what to do."

Sometimes that is true, but not always. It frequently happens in the early weeks that we simply do not know what to do. Despite all our sensitivity and attachment, we have no idea what is wanted. And because of the intensity of our involvement, the crying distresses us far more than anyone else. Mothers struggling with this frustration often begin to sense frustration in their babies' cries, too, as if the baby is saying, "Do something! You're supposed to know. Do something fast to help me!" So tension builds.

At first we feel sorry and go to any lengths to discover and relieve the source of the crying. We are patient, soothing, and worried. But if the crying persists, and we've gone through all the last resorts, worry begins to turn to fatigue, and out of the strain comes anger and impatience. Why is the baby so ungrateful and re-jecting when we've done absolutely everything we know to do? Anger alternates with terror and guilt—What have we done wrong?—causing the lowest hours of the first several weeks. There is little more upsetting than listening to your own inconsolable in-fant cry.

Unfortunately, newborns frequently cry a lot, much more than any new mother expects, and the reasons for their crying are often obscure. Not only do *we* not know at times, but no one knows why. What it probably boils down to is that things out in the real world aren't nearly so cozy as they were inside where sound was muffled, temperature never varied, there were no hard surfaces, hunger or gas pains did not exist, and where the baby was gently rocked and constantly provided with close contact. If we could duplicate all those things now, maybe the baby wouldn't cry, but though we try, we can't do it completely, and so the baby has to adjust. As baby and mother adjust, there is crying on both sides.

> "Since nursing her is usually the one sure way to soothe her, when problems arise (say she refuses to go on, yet acts hungry and screams), I become incredibly frustrated. 'Oh, the last resort is gone. What do I do now?' I say in tears."

> "It seems like there is always an element of guilt, or feeling something's wrong with me, when she cries and I can't figure out why."

It takes time to learn about the baby's needs, and any advice we get from books or other people must be evaluated as to whether or not we think it is suitable. Every baby is different, with different tolerances, moods, and limits. Some babies sleep a lot, eat heartily, and don't seem to fuss much. Other babies are awake a good deal, get too excited by stimulation, and dawdle at the breast. There are any number of combinations, and a good deal of what we have to learn involves discovering what our particular baby is like.

Though this process of learning about a baby's personality begins right away, it takes weeks and months until we can work with instead of against it. Usually mothers are surprised at *whatever* their babies are like. All of the fantasies during pregnancy—that infants sleep a lot, that they cry when they want something we can definitely supply, that they eat in ten minutes and immediately fall back into a sound sleep, and that they entertain themselves happily all the rest of the time, leaving us hours to read, cook or do other projects—all of these bubbles are burst. There is disillusionment that babies, in general, are not nearly so accomodating; and often there is initial misunderstanding and worry about our own particular child.

If the baby cries a lot and seems tense and high strung—when we are not that way at all—we begin to wonder how the baby got like that. We worry that we are doing something wrong, did something wrong from the very beginning. If the baby doesn't eat well, seems withdrawn and quiet, we are sure that the child senses some deep psychological block to motherly love deep within us, of which we are not consciously aware.

It's hard enough abandoning our cozy expectations and figuring out exactly what the baby needs without overlaying it all with worry and guilt. This is the beginning of a relationship between strangers, each with individual differences, and each has to do some adjusting. We're doing things with as much ease and love as we can muster in these new circumstances, and the baby will adapt as we adapt. To worry about why the baby is a certain way is fruitless, though we probably won't stop doing it. The baby was born that way, and our task is to relate to this individuality as sensitively as possible.

What finally gets us through the adjustment is simply our unique attachment to the baby. Gradually, as we learn more about her temperament and special needs, we can start to figure out the best ways around whatever is upsetting to the baby, and at the same time provide the sorts of comforts the baby seems to enjoy.

> *"All the difficult aspects were purely physical except one. I couldn't figure out what to do with her while she was awake! I fed her, changed her, held her, but I didn't know what else she needed. It took a reassuring mother to show me what to do—which was basically to leave her to explore her tiny universe alone for a while."*

*"The minute I'd put him down even in the
earliest days, he would begin to howl. He wanted to be
held or walked or rocked constantly unless he was
asleep. And he didn't sleep much. I could not even go
to the bathroom without having him on my lap. I'd put
him in the front pack to cook. Someone else would
have to be in the house if I wanted to take a shower.
I'd assumed that, given enough to look at or the right
toys, kids could pretty much entertain themselves right
from the beginning. Only now has he started to play
by himself for fifteen minutes at a stretch, and he's
nearly two and a half."*

Unfortunately, the baby is a fickle teacher. Once we've discovered that the baby doesn't especially care for rocking chairs or that sort of motion, there comes a day when nothing works but that old neglected rocker. We might firmly believe that the baby likes the close contact of swaddling, only to find one day that it produces insulted protests. The baby's needs seem to change faster than even he or she can keep up with at this age, so both mother and baby are thrown into a fragile routine of trial, error, and hope.

If, however, we attempt to relieve crying quickly, the baby will eventually begin to associate our presence with comfort, and will begin to trust the environment a little more. The baby's "language" has been responded to, and the baby has learned that it will be cared for. As many books nowadays say, there is no such thing as spoiling a newborn, there is only an establishment of trust that the child builds on for the rest of its life. If the baby knows that the world outside its body is a caring one, then the lesson has been learned that it's worthwhile to reach out, and life gets a little easier for us, too.

*"Throughout the first year the same pattern would
recur, I would have a period of anxiety that would last
a few days, because the baby had just started*

something new that was usually exciting, but that I would, nevertheless, have to reorient myself around. After my reorientation, everything would be great for a while. Then without warning, things would go haywire again. It would take me awhile to realize that something new was happening with him, and that I would have to adjust. The first weeks were the hardest that way, because I didn't know what in the world was going on, and it seemed like there was something new every other day."

Daily Care and Sleeping

Absolutely no new mother expects the complete shock she experiences at suddenly having to learn a myriad of new rituals and routines that consume literally all her waking hours and many of the hours she wishes she were sleeping. Whoever realized before that bathing an infant was such a delicate procedure or that one could feel nervous and inept doing it? Rashes appear and disappear magically. The baby is scratching itself, but how does anyone trim such micro-fingernails? The umbilical stump looks oozy. Is that a sign to call the doctor? No one had mentioned that light and air heal diaper rashes faster than medicines. Why does the baby hiccough so much? The baby falls asleep at the breast after screaming to be fed five minutes before, and will scream again in another half hour. But when we change the diaper to wake the baby up, there are screams through the whole procedure. The baby can't stand bright lights so we considerately pull the shades, but then don't see the puddle of spit-up that causes a rash on the baby's cheek. Which clothes are the most practical for changing diapers, for warmth, for handling?

It's all a foreign country with signs in a strange language. We have to pass through it, there's no way around, and everyone has the same problems. It's a solitary journey which each mother has to make more or less by herself. There are a few considerate people along the way who offer help (Dr. Spock is good), but mostly it's a difficult passage. To come through it knowing what works best, most efficiently and pleasantly for all concerned, is a minor victory—of which we may be hardly aware, in a month's time. We only know that gradually the routine things are a little more familiar.

Unfortunately, there is no way to ease this shock of not knowing. We can only realize that all mothers experience the same time-consuming, exhausting misgivings, lack of knowledge, and mistrust of their abilities. No one has any pat answers, because everything has to be worked out individually to suit our and our babies' needs. If this doesn't sound formidable, remember that throughout this adjustment stage we are robbed of sleep.

Sleep, which we had taken for granted before, now becomes a precious state. Studies have shown that infants sleep an average of sixteen hours and twenty minutes out of twenty-four hours in the first week, and that it is arranged in short periods almost equally distributed between day and night; approximately eight hours at night and eight hours during the day.[6] But that means that eight hours in every twenty-four, newborn babies are awake—and at random times around the clock. Even the researchers admit that within this "average" are wide individual differences,[7] and most mothers think their babies are awake more than this.

For new mothers, it's an unwelcome surprise to have the baby awake so long and so frequently. Part of this time they are eating, part of it they are crying, part of it they are just being quietly alert; and all of these things happen as easily at three o'clock in the morning as at three o'clock in the afternoon. Of necessity we have to adjust our schedules to theirs, and still that isn't enough, since we are not used to sleeping in short spurts so randomly distributed.

This sleeping (or lack of sleeping) pattern in the early weeks is one of the hardest adjustments, and it affects the emotions to no slight extent. Not only is it depressing just to think of never getting a full night's sleep for months, but it also leaves us ragged, never quite feeling at our best, or able to engage in many social activities for fear of the repercussions of exhaustion for the next couple of days. Many mothers feel that they can't concentrate and consequently have trouble remembering things.

In this continual context of not having one of our basic needs met, we can spiral down into depression. Then everything seems bleak and worthless. Small strains are insurmountable, tiny errors unforgivable. For many of us this is the first time we've ever felt such fatigue, that exhaustion turns into despair. Yet at this point there may be no awareness of fatigue, just a profound feeling of hopelessness. Sleep is the cure.

> *"I periodically become overwhelmed and start to cry, but that's almost always when I'm tired. Then I just have to tell myself to stop thinking and go to bed. Then I almost always feel amazingly better after a rest."*

Not Knowing

Everything is so new and overwhelming for at least the first month that we are completely absorbed by it. Often, we are shocked at the amount of work and time it takes to care for the baby. We certainly never expected it to be this way. We are worried and preoccupied by the things that we don't understand but which seem to affect the child so much at times. And we are tempted to think that it isn't this way for everyone else who becomes a mother for the first time.

It's frustrating that there are no definitive answers and that things are always changing. We are conviced at times that we're not doing things correctly that if we only had a little more experience or patience or intuitive feeling, things would be easier. Surely there are other new mothers who handle things much better, we muse.

That simply isn't so.

All new mothers are at times confused and overwhelmed, exhausted and worried, loving and insecure. We all learn as we go, doing the best we can, and there are few, if any shortcuts. It's hard, sometimes nerve-wracking, relentless work. But though it seems interminable as we're going through it, it doesn't actually last that long. Soon there are new problems and even greater rewards.

"Basically, after four-and-a-half months, I've finally realized how vital it is to rely on instinct. There may be no true 'mother instinct,' but there is certainly some intuitive process that guides me in finding the best way to keep my baby comfortable and stimulated. I guess it comes down to a commitment to trust myself, to rely on me. If I were to give advice to any new mother, it would simply be: Trust yourself!"

Suggested Reading:

Infants and Mothers, by T. Berry Brazelton

The First Twelve Months of Life, by Princeton Center for Infancy and Early Childhood

Baby and Child Care, by Benjamin Spock

What Now? A Handbook for New Parents, by Mary Lou Razdilsky and Barbara Banet

THE COUPLE

As a new mother interacts with her baby, the relationship she shares with her husband is inevitably transformed. Initially, the parental couple glows in the novel ectasy of the birth and the child that they share. Some of this precious excitement will linger for months, but too soon the difficulties of adjustment intervene. Like a molecule adding a new atom, the basic structure is irreversibly altered in a process that requires energy and progresses through a state of imbalance. It's the natural imbalance we will focus on here—the fears and worries that beset any two people as they shed their identity as a childless couple and become parents.

Expectations and the Liberation Movements

Today's husbands, who have shared household chores before the baby's birth, also expect to participate to a large degree in child care. This attitude has probably been discussed between the partners, and each expects that the job of child rearing will be lightened because they both will be sharing the burden. The liberation movements for both men and women have begun challenging the traditional roles of father as breadwinner and mother as housewife and chief of child care. We are sensitive to the ideas that men can take care of children as well as women can and that limiting a woman to the motherhood role is unfair and destructive.

Still, there are certain realities of which we are only partially aware, or which we only partially admit to ourselves before the baby's birth. First, *someone* has to earn a living, and most often it is the man who continues his job, while the woman opts to stay at home for a while with the baby. This is, of course, a free choice. Usually, the woman is glad to have some time at home. Nevertheless, that places us within the traditional context, though increasing numbers of women are returning to work within a few weeks of the birth. (See Chapter Seven—"Combining Work and Motherhood.")

Second, we as mothers feel so much closer to the baby than we think our husbands do that we are doubly glad to be at home. We never expected we would mistrust his handling of the child or his judgments, and yet, it is not uncommon to feel that he is not as sensitive or doesn't respond as quickly to the baby's cries or needs. It is surprising to us that we are so protective and so desirous of taking care of the baby ourselves, when we had expected to be able to share the chores willingly. Thus, we thrust ourselves and our husbands even further into the traditional maternal-paternal roles.

There is nothing inherently wrong with this structure, except that if we had expected—with "liberated" consciousness—to manage child care differently than our parents had, one of the first strains in the relationship with our husbands might develop around this issue. We feel resentful, and they feel guilty. The liberation movements have sensitized us, but not yet freed us. (See also Chapters Five and Six for more about resentments.)

"I would like to be working part-time, and I would like Peter to be taking care of the baby while I'm working. I trust him more than anyone else to give her the loving attention I feel she needs and deserves. But I don't think Peter wants to spend more time at home. No matter how precious babies are they can be boring at times. I've heard Peter say, 'I just couldn't spend twenty-four hours a day every day at home.' Then, when I suggest I should work a couple of days a week Peter says, 'There's nothing more important than raising children.' I don't think the two statements are contradictory for him. I think Peter feels the way I do, that raising children is the most important thing. I just wish we could do it more together, as I'd hoped we would."

"Since Bill is working outside of the home and I'm not, I probably do about two-thirds of the child care. But he helps with her a lot when he is at home. He's really good with her (at times better than I am since he doesn't get saturated with the primary responsibility).

"I wouldn't want our roles to be reversed (me working full-time and him staying at home with the baby all the time), and I don't wish I were working now. But I am looking forward to returning to work part-time next year. I miss teaching at times, and returning to work will be good since I won't be so totally preoccupied with the baby."

Structural Changes in the Relationship

"The inevitable changes in the husband and wife will, in turn, alter the marriage relationship and place strains on it until a new equilibrium can be established."[1]

"A baby's presence exerts a consistent and persistent domination over the outer and inner lives of every member of a household. Because these members must reorient themselves to accommodate his presence, they must also grow as individuals and as a group. It is as true to say that babies control and bring up their families as it is to say the converse. A family can bring up a baby only by being brought up by him. His growth consists of a series of challenges to them to serve his newly developing potentialities for social interaction."[2]

Before the baby, the time at the end of a workday was free to be spent either individually or as a couple. There was a wide choice of things to do, and both husband and wife were probably busy with hobbies and social activities. Most likely an attempt was made to set aside some time in the week specifically to "be together." Maybe there was always Sunday morning to sleep late, have a leisurely brunch, read the newspaper, comment on personal as well as world events, make love, and go for a bike ride. Maybe one of the weekend evenings was reserved for dinner and a movie out. Surely there was the occasional vacation for relaxing and "getting close." No matter how hectic life was, there was that base in the other person. And that base was founded on a sort of "you-for-me and me-for-you" exclusive commitment. Priorities centered around maintenance of the relationship and pursuit of individual careers.

Having a baby means adding another priority—that of taking care of the child and becoming a family. It means introducing another person into the exclusivity of the mutual commitment. It means there will be much less time to spend just with each other. In addition, there are added strains in terms of increased daily responsibilities and worries. Each of the facets contributes to the basic restructuring of the husband-wife relationship. Frequently, couples experience this process of change as a drifting apart over the course of the first year, as if the baby is a kind of wedge between them. In one study, couples said "things were going well" between them 85% of the time during the pregnancy, but at five months postpartum "things were going well" only 65% of the time.[3] Let's look at the changes more closely.

First, there are two independent adults, who choose for their mutual pleasure to live together and to try to help each other in times of need. They have separate lives, but also a combined one. One could say that they resemble two circles that link. When the baby is born, they have a greater area of intersection. They care not only what happens in their own separate lives, but they also have a greater emotional investment in their combined life. Suddenly the couple is not just two adults who choose to be together; they are two adults with a priority to raise a happy child, by providing it with an atmosphere of love—a family. There is now a need for not only "couple time" but also, "family time."

Second, the quality of the intimacy the couple has shared changes. More and more of their quiet time together is spent talking about the baby or problems related to the baby. They might feel that fewer of their individual emotional needs are being met, because there is less time in their talks to open up as completely as before. The husband sometimes feels neglected because of all the affection and concern his wife lavishes on the child. He frequently cites the inability to discuss his work as a complaint. Or he says that he doesn't feel left out, but hopes that the mother will have more time for the marital relationship when the child is a little older.[4]

The wife, in return, feels guilty at not having as much energy to pour into the relationship with her husband as she used to have. For a while, the husband-wife relationship simply takes a back seat to the one developing with the child. Each one, after all, is cultivating a relationship with the newcomer, and both parents have to integrate those separate relationships into the evolving familial structure. They are no longer simply two people with an exclusive commitment to each other.

At the same time, the baby can illuminate areas of softness and subtlety in the husband-wife relationship that might have been eclipsed before. Seeing the other person in a new role can foster fresh appreciations and spark a deeper love. For some couples, struggling together through the trials and late nights of a baby's first year draws them together in new ways. And some couples, stagnating in the exclusivity of the husband-wife commitment, are refreshed and enlivened by opening up their relationsip to another loved one.

Most of us regret the loss of the old, familiar type of closeness, but are also grateful for the unexpected new feelings. As in any transition, there is both a loss and a gain.

Third, on a practical level there is just less time to spend together without the baby, fewer hours that can be devoted to strictly unworried relaxation and entertainment. Those quiet mornings of sleeping late together, leisurely lovemaking, and brunch are gone for a few years. Evenings out for dinner and a movie have to be meticulously arranged to coordinate babysitting with restaurant reservations and theater times. An afternoon of lying in the park in the sun together frequently becomes one parent sunning and feeling guilty while the other parent entertains the baby, and longs for a nap.

Fourth, there seems to be a lot more work to be done. Everything from tripled laundry to the perpetual stack of dishes in the sink to the general housekeeping that seems to be put off indefinitely. It is no wonder that, as a couple, life seems jumbled and difficult for a time.

Even so, things do improve gradually. Despite the initial hardships and strains, the subjects in many studies reported that their marriages were ultimately the same or improved by the birth of a baby.[5,6,7] They indicated that their lives together had been enriched and that they felt a greater commitment to one another. Psychiatrist Theodore Lidz describes well some of the reasons for this positive change:

"The conception of the child is an act of mutual creativity during which the boundaries between the self and another were temporarily eradicated more completely than at any time since infancy. The child can be a continuing bond forged by that creativity; a focus of mutual hopes, interests, and efforts; and a blending of two personalities as well as of genes. Whereas each parent grew up the product of different family lines with differing customs and identifying with different parents, they are now united by a child whose experiences they will share and with whom they both identify. We must also recognize that they have willingly or unwillingly been turned into parents, and here, as in other spheres of life, many persons grow through finding the abilities to meet the responsibilities that are thrust upon them."[8]

"As much as we loved the baby and felt that he had drawn us together in many new ways, we also regretted losing the intimacy of having just the two of us. It takes a lot more effort or a very special occasion to be romantic and just devote ourselves to pleasing the other one for a while. There are too many other demands or intrusions. I would say that we don't have the time to 'play' with each other as much any more. Our relationship has a more serious intimate side to it, which is good, but different."

"We are madly in love with each other since the baby was born. We have done something together neither of us could do separately, and each of us wanted to do it. We have also been enjoying the pleasures of this real live human being, so innocent and honest in his needs and gifts."

"The baby stressed my relationship with Michael in ways I never would have imagined—almost because she was such a good baby. I became totally involved with her. She took all my energy and, it seemed, my love as well. I didn't have anything left for my husband or anybody else, and I felt very guilty. This lasted for several months. I felt if I was left on my own I could have gone off and been in a mud hut—me and my baby—and I would have been perfectly happy."

"The main change in our relationship is that we have so little time for it. Meals, one of the main times we used to talk to each other, are always interrupted by the baby's demands. Even when the baby is sleeping many of our conversations center on how to cope with her latest problems. On the rare occasions when we go out together, we're usually tired from lack of sleep or just from dealing with her. I miss all the relaxed, spontaneous, fun times we used to have together.

"We do feel more dependent on each other. We just have to work as a team in order to relieve each other of the pressures of child care and simply in order to get a meal on the table and the dishes occasionally done. We have to and so support each other a lot when one or the other of us gets frustrated by the baby. When we're both at home, we have to delineate very clearly at times who is responsible for the baby right then. That requires a lot of clear communication."

Sex

Most couples are anxious to resume their sexual life after the delivery as a symbol of their continuing connectedness, and perhaps as an attempted return to their old way of relating. But there are many new, unforeseen problems that make this difficult and cause the couple to fear that they might have traded in their sexuality for a child. This is part of the couple's transition that hardly anyone discusses, even though one study found "sexual incompatibility" after the birth of the child listed as the leading problem by couples.[9]

There is, on the most practical level, the problem of "when." To attempt lovemaking when the baby is awake is to court frustrating interruptions; nothing withers desire so fast as listening to your baby screaming in the background. When the baby takes short naps, there are usually a hundred tasks to be done. At night both partners drop into bed exhausted, desiring nothing more than the pleasure of sleep. The energy required for lovemaking can seem formidable and totally unavailable.

Then there are other less-than-arousing aspects to sex now that may make the couple nostalgic for the easy familiarity of the past. Often, in the first weeks following the delivery, the wife fears admitting her husband to an area of her body that has so recently been traumatized. Many women don't want to experience any kind of sensation in the genital area for weeks and dread the first sexual encounter as much as they want it. Even after the episiotomy or bruises have healed, there can still be discomfort during intercourse because the nursing woman does not produce sufficient lubrication. (The lactating hormones seem to decrease it.) This added tightness or friction can bring back memories of the pain during and after delivery and cause the woman to avoid further sexual activity for a while.

Nursing mothers' breasts are sometimes tender. And many women dislike their husbands fooling around with what is a necessity for the child. Also, too much manipulation causes the milk to flow, and frequently, mothers begin to drip or spray at just the climactic moment, not the most erotic of occurrences.

Though the couple loves the child they have, they usually fear another pregnancy and baby so soon after the first. Effective contraception takes on immense proportions, and since IUDs and pills are taboo at first, using other methods can increase the tension and mutual awkwardness of those first few sexual experiences after the birth. Nursing usually prevents ovulation but is not reliable enough to provide certainty.

These physical problems take on less significance as the couple learns to deal with them, and as the problems themselves diminish. Within a couple of months, vaginal discomfort during intercourse disappears or lubricants can be used to counteract the dryness. As nursing becomes a simple routine, the tenderness and concern about the breasts decreases; and compromises are worked out between husband and wife about sexuality and breast-feeding. The logistics of contraception become more familiar with each use.

One problem, however, which seems to continue for a longer time, and is often far more distressing, is the mother's apparent lack of interest in sex. Certainly there are women for whom this is not the case, (Masters and Johnson's sample of nursing women reported unchanged or increased sexual desire after the birth[10]), but many women feel little, if any sexual drive for months. Physiologic changes due to continued breast-feeding probably account for much of the lack of libido, although little research has been done on sexuality in early motherhood. Since the secretion of vaginal lubricants in a woman corresponds to the erection in a man, and the lactation hormones suppress lubrication, it would seem that hormones are at least partly the cause of decreased sexual drive. Furthermore, women report an increase in desire after the nursing has stopped—exactly when the desire returns, however, varies.

There is, no doubt, also an emotional component to decreased desire. We are in the early months so attached to our babies that we expend enormous amounts of physical affection and care on them. Not only do we enjoy doing this, but we also feel that they need it. We feel that our husbands, on the other hand, can make do for a time without our special attention.

Nevertheless, we may feel anxious and guilt-ridden that we cannot relate to our husbands in a sexual way. We are certain that they are resentful or hurt by being continually turned away. We may make sexual overtures and try very hard to enjoy the lovemaking, but more often than not, the experience is difficult for both partners, and we may become angry at our unresponsive bodies and disappointed husbands.

Most couples try to discuss and understand each other's point of view, and try to learn new ways to be affectionate which are less threatening to the wife. Each partner needs to reassure the other—because eventually the desire does return, almost always to its previous level, but it takes longer than most couples expect.

> *"I desperately needed affection and attention as if to replenish the supplies after I had been giving so much to the baby. And my husband did too, just to know that I still liked him. But I had no interest in sex at all. In fact, if he approached me in any sort of sexual way I would almost panic. Eventually, we worked out a plan that I could tolerate. We called it 'cuddling without fear.' If I was sure he had no designs on my body, I could relax and we could both enjoy just the simple closeness."*

> *"We had sex for the first time four weeks after the baby was born, and it was awful. I cried. I thought I had become frigid. I was scared it would hurt, and since I had no lubrication at all, it did. I thought perhaps sex had only been exciting to me before because I had always wanted to be pregnant, and that now I would never enjoy it again, never be independent from my mother role again."*

> *"We resumed sex at seven-and-a-half weeks postpartum. We had tried earlier but it hurt too much.*

And even at this time it hurt. I was a bit scared and wanted to get the first time over with, partly out of fear that I'd never get around to that first time.
Though I'd had sexual dreams before that, I still didn't feel very sexy or turned on. Even three months after the birth, sex was still painful, but beginning to be less so.

"Up until now my orgasms have been very mild or nonexistent, but that problem seems to be improving, too."

Evolution of Each Partner

Both the man and woman are changing and adapting to their new roles as parents, as well as adjusting as a couple. The wife, for instance, is probably having to adjust to being at home and being more dependent both financially and emotionally on her husband. The baby and the home become her focal interests, and she must change in certain ways to suit her new environment and job. In addition, she is trying to understand exactly what it means to be a mother. (See also Chapter Five, "Maturational Crisis" section.) The husband, at the same time, might be trying to discern how he is supposed to fit into the intimate relationship his wife and child have formed, and he might take a more serious look at his job and role as financial provider. It is a time of rapid personal growth for both new parents, and strains are inevitable as each tries to sort out and understand his or her new life.

It has been noted that each new parent has slightly different concerns that they focus on.[11] The wife, for instance, has been found to often feel "edgy" or upset—and that was her number one difficulty—whereas it did not even rank on the husband's list of problems. His first worry was over money. The same study found that while the wife was bothered by the "housekeeping not being as neat as it should be" (which was high on her list), the husband was disappointed in their "decreased contact with friends." The wife worried about her figure and appearance and reduced privacy for herself. These, too, were not among the husband's difficulties: he doubted his worth as a parent; disliked interference from the in-laws; and was annoyed by the meals being off schedule. None of those things were on the mothers' lists.

This revealing selection of non-intersecting emotional difficulties demonstrates how the spouses each work separately on the same task, that of becoming a parent. Because of the specific roles they fulfill and their differing degrees of involvement with the baby, they each have different needs and problems to work out individually. This further divides them while the adaptations are occurring. And since there is less time for expressing feelings, these adjustments are worked through more-or-less alone.

One conflict that often surfaces during this evolution concerns differing views about child care. And underlying this issue is the insecurity of each parent in their new roles. The mother seems to know the baby so well, that the father may begin to doubt that he really can care for the baby, because he sees the mother so much better equipped to handle various situations that arise. And she is of course the last resort with her ability to breast-feed when the baby is inconsolable.

Soon, he might find himself waiting to do anything until his wife gives instructions, and always deferring to her judgments. He can become, in short, an inadequate mother-substitute, instead of developing and respecting his own unique ways of handling the baby. Not only might he begin to resent this second-rate status, but it can also delay his own particular transition to fatherhood.

His wife, meanwhile, wishes for him to take more initiative and repsonsibility in the child care, but does not always see how she is inadvertently limiting his ability to do so. (Chances are she forcefully intervenes each time the baby needs attention in order to alleviate her own insecure feelings about mothering.) She thinks that he lets the baby go longer without changing a diaper, or allows more crying before picking the baby up, or misunderstands the baby's moods. As the wife moves in to compensate for his apparent insensitivity, she further hinders the husband's ability to learn or to do things in his own way.

Often, this situation lasts for a few months—until the father finally feels confident enough to assert his opinions or until the wife relinquishes enough responsibility. Each is eager to do a good job as a parent, of course, and each is also eager to strike the right balance with his or her partner. Differences of opinion about how things should be done need to be respected and discussed, and compromises need to be made. Ultimately, all of this explicitly working out of things is a healthy sign. For the husband begins to understand that his role as father is as special as his wife's role as mother, and that his is different from hers. He learns to relate to the baby in a way that is most comfortable for him and does not simply duplicate that of his wife.

The more responsibility fathers took, one study showed, and no matter what particular things they did, the more effective was their adjustment to fatherhood.[12] The wife, by admitting her husband into the relationship she has formed with the baby, frees herself somewhat physically and facilitates her own adjustment to what will eventually be the more permanent family structure. For the first year she may be a more special person to the baby; but increasingly, the child will become equally attached to, and needful of the father.

The husband and wife are separate individuals, and they will obviously have very different ways of relating to the baby. It is surprising how quickly and easily the baby understands this and begins to respond to them each uniquely.

One of the greatest pleasures a couple can share in their individual adjustments to parenthood is watching the other one interact with the baby in her or his own special way. It emphasizes the differences between them as parents and people. It gives them new reasons to love each other, and it provides the baby with a broader environment from which to learn about the world.

> *"I love watching him play with the baby or talk to him. He uses all new words and fantasies. I get tired of my same old ways, and I'm sure the baby does, too. Tom is wonderfully refreshing for him."*

> *"One new father I know accused his wife of 'hogging the baby.' When she finally realized that her husband's style of handling the baby, while different from hers was not harmful, then she relaxed and let him take over much more."*

The New Mother's Feelings About Relationship Problems

It is terribly frightening at times to feel that the relationship to our husband is shaky. We feel vulnerable anyway in the new role as mother. We feel physically undesirable with the extra pounds we've added, and we panic at the thought of how dependent we've become. If there were to be a major clash now with our husband, we would crumble.

We very much want things with him to be as they were *before*—when we felt stronger and more confident about the relationship. But that is impossible, and we may fear remaining forever in a state of quivering imbalance—that we'll never again be able to be as intimate and loving with him. In addition, we may feel that we have the primary reponsibility for maintenance of the relationship and of the new family. It has traditionally been the mother's task to keep all the family members happy and things running smoothly. We feel that we're not successful if we can't even adequately manage what was so easy before—the relationship with our man.

But with so much going on, it is not surprising that there may be misunderstandings and stresses. Every couple experiences them to varying degrees, and they keep changing as the baby changes.

Gradually, the couple works out methods of dealing with the strains as they come: patterns that worked once will probably work again. Underneath it all, they usually see that the basic love they shared has not changed; things do improve with time—and experience.

Suggested Reading:

Our Bodies, Ourselves, by The Boston Women's Health Book Collective

Ourselves and Our Children, by The Boston Women's Health Book Collective

How to Father, by Fitzhugh Dodson

The Father Book, by Alliance for Perinatal Research and Services, Inc.

CHAPTER FOUR

GRANDPARENTS

Having a child usually means seeing the grandparents more often than before. They are anxious to join the fun of seeing the baby grow and develop, and they know from experience how fast that happens. A sort of tentative, curious, mutual observation goes on at first between new parents and grandparents. The grandparents are curious about how their children will be as parents; this might be seen as sort of ultimate test of how *they* were as parents and of how much of their influence was carried over.

The new parents are interested in the effect the child will have on the grandparents, since grandparents are the one other set of people who are assumed to offer unquestioning, immediate love to the child. We as new parents are anxious for other people to appreciate and love our baby as we do. And so we are proud and hopeful as we offer the baby to them.

Besides curiosity, both parents and grandparents bring certain expectations to the first few encounters. Many new mothers find to their surprise that they had unconsiously hoped the child might bring the parents and grandparents closer together—that its very existence would smooth over previous difficulties. Another common expectation is that the grandparents might finally start treating the parents as equals. The parents offer the child as a kind of proof of their adulthood and responsibility, hoping the grandparents will accept them as grown-ups.

On their side, the grandparents have their own expectations. Most likely these are quite different from those of the parents, because their needs are different. Grandparents frequently see the grandchild as their link to the future. Their line will be carried on, and they might comment on how the child is similar to them in one way or another. Or they might expect the experience of parenthood to give the new parents greater appreciation and gratitude for the hardships they endured for their child.

Usually, everyone is pleased and proud initially. There is a common focus for attention and conversation, and parents and grandparents might get along better than they have in years. But in some cases the different expectations of parents and grandparents can cause frustration and disappointment.

Forgetting the early struggles of parenthood, the grandparents might think us too nervous or cautious. Times and practices have changed, and they might disapprove of some of the new things we do. We are acutely aware of their reactions to us, and since we're probably unsure of ourselves, their disapproval might hurt much more than we had anticipated.

They might disappoint us by not falling into the role of doting grandparents immediately. Or they might express their affection in ways that irritate us and, we are sure, the baby as well.

Slowly, as we become more confident and they begin to understand our style, they begin to seem less disapproving about our parenting. No doubt they are reassured in time that we are doing okay, and that we need to do it our own way. We also become accustomed to the way they do or do not show their love to the child.

In terms of hopes for greater closeness with our parents, there is usually little change in the actual relationship in the long run. Despite the immediate flurry of emotions and hopes surrounding the baby's birth, both parents and grandparents eventually come to accept that things aren't going to change that much, even though the final card has been played.

"Nobody talks much about how a person has to learn to be a grandparent, but that was really the case with my father-in-law. The first time he met our son he wore a face mask, (to keep away germs—he is a doctor), he inspected him like a pediatrician would, and he commented on his apparent health. He didn't once hold him during the entire three-day visit. I was angry and amused at the same time. It was obvious he was nervous and could only relate to his grandson in his habitual, professional way. He has softened a great deal, and as other grandchildren have come into the family, he has obviously come to enjoy cuddling them, as he learned what it means to be a grandparent."

"I was very hesitant to invite either set of grandparents to come up soon after the birth. After all, our visits with them for years had been emotionally trying ... Another reason we didn't want to invite our parents was that in our ignorance of a baby's demands, we simply had no idea how much we would need

help. However, we finally decided to invite each set of grandparents for separate weeks, and they were both great. We felt close to them as we all helped care for the baby.

"The occasion made us feel closer to our parents than we had since we were children!"

Child into Parent

"I still carried with me a sense of being a child myself—at age thirty—and with a shock I was transformed into a mother and caretaker."

All of us, to a certain extent, think of ourselves even in adulthood as children. Deep down we still feel that we're twelve or seven; we are still a little shaken by authority figures and lack confidence in certain "adult" situations. We assume that one day the magic sensation that we have truly reached the age we are will sweep over us—and we will start acting like we thought those thirty-year-olds acted when we were growing up. But it doesn't happen. Even very old people describe the same feeling. Yes, they are eighty, but it's hard to believe. They never thought eighty-year-olds felt this way. Underneath it all, they still feel like children.

Having a baby highlights the fact that we are now at a stage in life when we are supposed to be feeling the way we thought our parents felt—confident, independent, competent. It's a surprise to find that those self-assured feelings don't just come with the baby. Not only that, we are giving so much to the baby that we probably feel in need of nurturance ourselves. Possibly for the first time in years, we look to our parents for guidance and love.

We still hope and expect that they are capable of understanding our needs and will help out in just the right way at the crucial moment. This hope is usually founded on romantic memories of our parent's love. Everyone cherishes such memories, though we might have grown away from them, and we're now often quite different from our parents in our life values and pleasures.

But with the birth of a baby, there is a tendency to feel close to our own parents again—to our mother especially. Suddenly, we can comprehend what she went through for us! Here we are giving our all to an infant just as she did for us, and it seems a precious and appropriate time to rekindle that childhood reverence and love for her.

But to rekindle that childhood admiration is to become a child again. Yes, we are in reality still her child, and there are times when we might want to retreat to the shelter of her arms. But we are also grown women, and most of the time, we want to be distinct individuals—separate from her. These conflicting feelings around the time of the birth of the child can be painful, and yet are important.

We are finally relinquishing most of our fortunate position as a child in favor of being a parent. We have moved from one life position to another. And we experience at this point a sort of identity crisis; "Who am I, actually?" "Where in life am I?"

For our mothers, the same thing is occurring. If this is her first grandchild, she is moving into grandparenthood, and most likely she has ambivalent feelings about that as well. For one thing, she is probably vicariously reliving through her daughter her own pregnancies and deliveries and her own early mothering.

This kind of re-experiencing of the past can be very pleasurable for her as she recalls the good aspects of the past while not actually burdened with child care. Much like her daughter, she probably glorifies the past and desires an uncomplicated, profound love for her daughter again. However, if she has experienced rejection by her daughter in recent years—or if she is simply disarmed by the cuteness of babies—she may find it easier to shower her love on the grandchild. This is likely to be enjoyable, too—since this grandmotherly affection is unburdened by the doubts and anxieties that plagued her as a young mother.[1]

At the same time, she clearly understands the implications of grandmotherhood in the life cycle. She is no longer in her prime as her daughter—at the height of reproductive and parental influence—is now. She is, on the down-swing, forced to take a back seat and watch. She might feel proud of her daughter's ability to be a good mother, but she also feels replaced. She might feel fulfillment at seeing her daughter established and happy in a family of her own making, but she also feels loss. The daughter's original family is no longer of primary importance; and though this might have been true for the daughter for some time, the birth of the baby tends to bring it home.

Relationship with Mother and Family of Origin

Most of our feelings about grandparents seem to focus on our own mothers. All of the idiosyncracies, attitudes, and values about mothering that we acquired as little girls come to the surface now.

We are surprised at how we automatically do things as she did them—or how in reaction, we do things in order to be precisely different from her. Both ways, the mothering we received is consciously and unconsciously very much a part of us and part of our style. We haven't identified so closely with our mothers since we were small. As psychoanalyst Therese Benedek puts it: "The empathy of the mother for her child originates in the experiences of her early infancy which are reanimated by the emotions of the current experience of motherhood."[2]

For some of us this is pleasurable—to feel that we are a link in a chain of love extending through the generations of women in our family. We like to think that we will be introducing our children into all that richness and that they will benefit from it, as we did. Others of us are distressed by similarities between ourselves and our mothers, because we see in ourselves things we did not particularly like about her. These women may grieve and be angry again for not having had what they thought was a good mother.

There can be dread at the possibility of passing her characteristics on to the child.

Either way, this close link to our mothers is highly charged. Having a baby is a direct route back to our own childhoods; and anything which can elicit the past so effectively is bound to be powerful and laden with feelings. Ultimately, it probably aids the adjustment to motherhood to relive our experiences with our mothers, and to work through and resolve, to some degree, our fundamental issues with her.[3]

Not so surprisingly, we tend to approach that potent woman—our mother—carefully. If we respect her opinions, we often desire her support and constructive guidance, but we also try to guard against too much advice. Too much advice stifles our own feelings of competence.

In addition to wanting both support and autonomy from her, there is also a mixture of guilt and appreciation. We feel guilty for not understanding before the extent of what she did for us, and for rejecting her in recent years, as we struck out on our own. But we also feel appreciative of her compassion for us and usually desire to be more intimate with her in order to share this common experience.

With our fathers, a similar sort of process is occurring, but it is probably not so obvious or disturbing to us. We might have an idealized vision of what our fathers were like or else we might totally dismiss their efforts as fathers. In either case, those subtle memories influence the way we hope our husbands will be with the baby.

Since the expectations don't involve us directly (we are not trying to imitate or be different from his style), it might take longer to realize that they are, nevertheless, there. And they will probably come up unexpectedly in the months ahead in the form of wishes or demands that we make upon our husbands.

The families we grew up in, obviously, have made indelible

impressions upon us, all of which we examine and deal with when we start our own families.

> *"I feel a greater closeness to my mother. I recognize her as my mother, and I recognize that some of the new things I'm learning and feeling may be similar to some of what my mother learned and felt during her time as a mother. I have a greater sense of forgiving."*

> *"After the baby's birth, my mother amazed me with her ability to support me and give tips on the baby's care without ever making me feel inadequate. We talked together and shared more of our usually hidden selves than we ever before had, and I felt appreciative and close to her.*
> *"Barriers seemed to fall miraculously as we talked easily about breast-feeding, the birth, or my continued bleeding.*
> *"I had never realized before how much my mother enjoyed babies. When she said, 'I just love little babies so much and I guess that's partly why we had so many,' I learned something new and wonderful about her. I could imagine her young, pretty, and enthusiastic as she cared for me and the other children, and that thought somehow made me feel more loved in retrospect."*

> *"My mother died suddenly six weeks before Josh was born. She had been excited about the pregnancy, and one of my overwhelming regrets was utter dejection that she never got to meet him. But that was as much sadness in relation to her future grandmothering than I would let myself admit at the time. I should have admitted more.*

"She was with me in everything. I tried to imitate what I remembered of her mothering in everything I did. But it was hardly ever conscious. I didn't let it be until after a year my grief really hit me, and all those suppressed, unthought-about issues of her motherliness in relation to mine came out."

"I feel a general sense of forgiveness of my parents since Alan was born. Somehow, through all their mistakes and selfishness I sense the love all parents must feel. I also have more kindness because of my labor and delivery and pregnancy itself. It's not easy, babies don't come easy. I didn't come easy."

THE SECOND MONTH

The time between three days and three months postpartum is "probably one of the hardest periods in a woman's lifetime."[1] While the daily routine has become familiar and less threatening by the time the second month begins, many realizations—some about our bodies, and other psychological ones—are just surfacing.

We have discussed the new mother's altering relationship with her husband and her parents—changes which begin in the early postpartum days and continue throughout the first year and beyond. We have looked at her budding relationship with her baby. But at some point, perhaps as early as the second month the new mother must also begin to look closely at herself.

She must look at how she is changing: at what she used to be, and at the person she is becoming. Most of us don't do this consciously, we just become aware sometime down the line that something has changed in us. But we feel that something is happening because of a whole range of ambivalent, often negative emotions that begin to arise.

It should be said that while most women seem to experience many of these conflicts and issues in their adjustment to motherhood, personal change and growth is as different as the individuals who go through it. Also, many changes occur in response to the baby's development, and each baby has its own pace. Thus, there can be widely varying times when we feel these things. The reason for discussing the changes on a month-by-month basis, is to emphasize that the adjustment takes place over a very long period of time. Our feelings are constantly shifing and developing as new realizations and understandings occur to us throughout the first year and the years to come.

It Couldn't Be This Hard for Everyone!

At some point in the second month or a little later, most of us realize that we are still having a very difficult time. We are still often tired and unable to accept much responsibility beyond child care and minimal care for ourselves. As happy as we feel about the baby—much more happy and in love than we had ever thought we would be—we also feel depressed sometimes, or bored or angry at the position we've found ourselves in.

Yet, we fear that expressing these more negative emotions would reflect badly on our mothering (i.e., we don't love the child enough, or we're not good mothers). So we tend to suppress or ignore these feelings. We assume that other mothers don't feel such things and are well-adjusted, delighted with their offspring, even slim again. It is worrisome that life still seems to be hard for us. This can lead to the feeling that we are basically inadequate.

Everyone has a difficult time! But hardly anyone admits it, or admits the depth and extent of their feelings. This can isolate us even more and make us feel even more inadequate. Besides the myth that mothers never experience boredom or doubts about themselves, there is also in our society a high premium on self-sufficiency. From the pilgrims to the frontiers-people, the ideal has always been the strong, independent individual who squarely met any challenge. The degree to which we fit that ideal is somehow an unspoken measure of our worth.

Most new mothers feel a need to act as though they are unfazed by the whole demanding experience, that they are taking it all in stride, that they are in control. To the outer world, the mother presents the acceptable, admirable qualities of devotion to the child, efficiency, and love of the new life. But underneath, she may be troubled and sometimes tearful about not feeling confident.

The dual myths of perfect motherhood and pride in self-sufficiency have us in thrall. We are, in fact, neither bad mothers nor weak individuals to be feeling so lost. We are merely normal.

Now is the time, if we haven't already, to reach out to other people, other new mothers preferably, who will understand and accept our feelings, and with whom we can commiserate. Often just knowing that other people have similar problems and feelings helps a lot. We begin to realize we are not so alone or incapable.

But sometimes even this is hard. Talking to mothers who are trying to be perfect can make us feel even more inadequate, and it's impossible to break through their defenses! They are stubbornly sticking to their act of being in control, or maybe they are just having a good day. It's important to find a person or a group that places a high value on honesty and sharing feelings as openly as possible.

Body Changes

By two months postpartum we yearn for our old bodies, and are scared that perhaps we'll never again be as thin and taut as before.

In some ways, the shape of our bodies seems symbolic of all we've given up and how much we have to come to terms with. Physically and psychologically we'll never be the same again, we think, though this is only partially true. Except for some minor differences, our bodies will return to normal. But it does take time, much longer than we had anticipated, and in that period we tend to feel undesirable and sloppy and out of control.

Most women are upset by the paunches they carry around, forcing them back into the maternity clothes they hoped they would be able to burn. The ligaments, muscles, and skin that had been so distended don't snap back like rubber bands. It takes *at least* six weeks—but usually longer—for these structures to return to something like normal.[2] And it takes much longer still for the abdominal wall to resume completely its pre-pregnancy state.

Exercise is the only way to bring about a total recovery. And even though we know it is wise to start off exercising gradually, it can be a shock to discover that doing just one partial sit-up is nearly impossible at first. Nevertheless, if we stick to it, our abdomens will approximate their usual state within a few months. The stretch marks fade to silvery-white, but never totally go away. The brown line fades almost totally.

It also takes time to reduce the weight gained. In this era of liberal weight gain during pregnancy, there are usually ten to twenty pounds to lose after delivery. If we've never been overweight before, the idea of having to take off that many pounds can be depressing. Usually at six weeks when the obstetrician declares us normal again, we groan that we still don't fit into any of our old clothes, and that we are flabby in all the wrong places. At this point it is wise to invest in a couple of bigger-than-average outfits just for morale's sake, and patiently begin to work off the weight. If you're breast-feeding, you can't diet much. You and the baby need all the important calories you can get. But the combination of cutting out sweets and nursing usually will take the pounds off.

The onset of menstruation varies tremendously. Sometimes it doesn't happen until weaning begins, other times it happens within a couple of months of delivery. Ovulation can occur at any time though, and as ovulation precedes a period, you cannot know when you're fertile again. Contraception should be used as soon as you recommence having sex, if you don't want to conceive. About six weeks after weaning, breasts return to their same size but are not as firm. At that point the physical return to normalcy is finished.

> *"I felt frustrated by how long it took for my normal energy to return—about five or six weeks. I'd never been a convalescent before and was longing to be able to zip around as usual."*

> *"In so many ways I keep wanting my own old familiar body back and it's taking so long. (That's a disadvantage of breastfeeding.)"*

> *"I was prepared to be 'back to normal' in three weeks. In three weeks I was still in maternity clothes, pale as a ghost, and tired! It took me more like three months! I feel fine now, although still a little loose around my waist and stomach."*

"Maturational Crisis"

Even though our bodies return to something close to their old condition, our lives and minds are permanently altered by having a child. In those aspects we truly will *never* be the same again. And it is this awareness that we begin to glimpse in the second month.

There is still enough newness and chaos that we tend to think life will get back to normal, as soon as the little houseguest starts behaving a bit more civilly.

This does not occur. The baby will be a demanding, non-contributing member of the family for a long time, and there is nothing to do but get used to it, adapt, change.

As in adolescence (around menstruation) and middle age (around menopause), we have to adjust to a new self-image. And as in those transitions, we have definite physiological changes[3] to contend with. The hormonal and physical alterations that our bodies have undergone in the pregnancy, and that are still being resolved, contribute to an overall "crisis."

The "crisis" or turning point—a period of instability—is leading us to a new life phase, when we will understand and accept our new, parental role. A psychologist/nurse, interested in her own adjustment during major transition phases in her life described her impressions of these times:

"It seemed that some of my feelings must be very similar to what an adolescent experiences . . . There were times during a transition phase when it was difficult to think clearly enough to follow a set of directions and solve problems such as balancing a checkbook or completing income tax forms. There were times when I felt as though my life were not my own, but instead belonged to all those who claimed me, such as my child, my husband, my parents, my teachers, and my employer. I had the feeling at these times that nothing I could do would really help. I could only wait for time to change things. I felt as if the change had to be within me and could not come from the outside. There did not seem to be any real unity among all the activities I was trying to accomplish. At these times I believe I was experiencing changes in my identity . . . ."[4]

What are some of the factors that lead to the disintegration of self-image and identity change? First of all, for many women there is a shift of emphasis from career to home and child. Either they are suddenly at home after being a working woman for years, or they are still working outside the home, but have added the responsibility of a child. Those who continue to work have to cope with guilty feelings at leaving the child, and have to divide their attention and concern between work and home. It's an exhausting balancing act to take care of both, and often women feel that they are neglecting one for the sake of the other. (See also Chapter Seven, "Combining Work and Motherhood" section.)

For those of us who choose to stay home with a child, there are different problems. We have to narrow our focus from the job, social relationships, and freedom of time and movement we enjoyed as working women to the relatively isolating and restrictive environment of home and child care. On the one hand, we are very glad to be able to spend time with our babies, to watch their growth and daily accomplishments, to know that we are giving as much as we can. Sometimes we feel lucky to be able to go out and enjoy a beautiful day, shop or visit a museum when we know others don't have such freedom. But on the other hand, we miss adult company. We long for those times when we could just hop in the car and go without having to remember to take diapers, clothes, infant seat, stroller, pacifier, and blankets.

Since we are home anyway, and housework fits so well with child care as it's so eminently interruptable, we may take on more and more of the household chores and cooking than we did as working women. We like our husbands to be able to spend time with us as a family when they come home instead of doing chores, so we take over their old "half" of the work. Besides, it's a challenge and a matter of pride to manage both housework and child care, so we end up doing most or all of it. Thus, we have effectively made the switch from career woman to mother and housewife.

Just because we've done it, does not necessarily mean that we are totally in love with the situation though. The repetitiveness of household routines, washing things only to dirty them again and always seeing something else that needs to be done is dulling and frustrating at times. Society's low evaluation of staying at home drags on us; and even though we look with pride on the small advances our babies are making, we know deep down that these are their accomplishments, not ours.

If we've had a career before, we find that we still define ourselves in those terms if someone asks, since we're reluctant to admit to being "just" a housewife and mother. We might feel guilty that we're not as dedicated to our profession as other mothers who return to work quickly. Maybe we think that we're using the baby as an excuse to stay home because we weren't doing so well at work anyway. Underneath may be the feeling that we are basically very traditional and unliberated after all! And the women's movement has, in general, reinforced this low opinion of mothers and housewives.

Studies show that the mother's role change is in fact one of the most difficult and long-lasting aspects of postpartum adjustment.[5] [6] Whereas personal insecurity, such as inexperience with kids or the fact that this is the first child, were relatively short-lived, the emotional difficulties related to role conflicts were thornier and, over the long run, were linked to difficult postpartum depressions more than other factors. Whether a woman continues to work outside the home or stays at home full-time, she has to make a major adjustment vis a vis her career. And this ultimately relates to her self-image.

> "My lifestyle has changed drastically, from full-time, career-oriented woman to full-time, mother-oriented. I can't help but feel this changes the way my husband relates to me and changes the way I see myself.
> "I am frightened by what the long-term effects of this might be, but I feel a tremendous tug to stay with our baby. Along with this comes greater dependency,

financial, emotional, and physical—none of it comfortable.

"I never thought of life-insurance coverage on my husband before, but suddenly that seems essential. The dependency has definitely increased. In some ways, as uncomfortable as it was in the beginning, it has taught me that I can trust and that has been a growing experience for me."

"After the first month, the parade of visitors was finished. I thought that left alone all day to care for the baby, I might grow bored and lonely. This fear also prompted the postpartum reaction: it was not depression, but rather the need to consciously sort out my life, making room for this new role as 'mother.' "

A second important adjustment concerns a lack of time for ourselves: the baby's needs intrude constantly and unpredictably. And our own needs frequently go unmet. If formerly we enjoyed reading or elaborate cooking or daily exercising, there now often isn't time for those things on a regular basis. We may feel frustrated and controlled, and we have to learn that we are not just individuals with only our own needs to consider. We are mothers as well, and that means less than half as much time and attention for ourselves. Personal wishes have to be adapted.

This usually means curtailing our interests and activities and narrowing our range of pleasures. We do this as a matter of course, because we love the baby and because it is the responsible thing to do. We do it trusting we are trading one set of pleasures for another; but we don't know much about that new lifestyle yet, and so there is natually some, even considerable, regret at what we are giving up. Our self-image is becoming more focused on mothering instead of on our previous interests.

This is not to say that we have given up personal interests permanently and will always be short of time for ourselves. But in the second month and for quite a while, the baby's needs are great. In the second half of the first year, things settle a bit and there is more time. Even so, there is not as much free time as there was before, and as the baby changes parenting constantly takes on new faces and makes new demands. We must make room for this new part of ourselves.

> *"I would stare at my Virginia Woolf books on the shelf, remembering my academic days, and long to just sit and read one of them again, devour and enjoy it, like I used to. But I knew there was no time for that, and besides most of the reason I wanted to do that was to hop back into that old me for a while. I think I would have felt out of place there, but that nostalgia and mourning would creep over me every few months."*

We sometimes resent that our husbands' lives have not changed so drastically and suddenly as ours. Maybe they spend a little less time at work, maybe they have cut down on their interests and activities. But still they are the ones who enjoy the freedom of walking out of the house every day and into a stimulating world of people. Husbands usually don't pack the diaper bag or sit in a back room with the baby during a party. They are not so quickly worried about sniffles or abnormal crying. They do not feel the guilt about going back to work as we do.

At first maternity is a more fundamentally life-altering step than paternity. Mothers have to jump in immediately and wholeheartedly, while fathers have a little more time to test the water and ease in. The changes are probably as profound in both eventually, but the crisis for mothers comes earlier and is more dramatic and disorienting. At least two studies underscore this fact in finding that women have a harder time at first[7] and that when one partner was more upset about something or other, it was always the wife.[8]

"I used to resent Michael mostly because I was more tied to our baby due to breast-feeding, and that made me more responsive to his needs. Michael seemed kind of aloof. He became more involved later on, and it feels quite comfortable in that regard now."

"Though I grow desperate for breaks from the baby, I feel guilty at times about asking Bill to babysit when he's home. After all, he has his job, and it doesn't seem fair to saddle him with a lot of child care too, giving him no time for himself. He protests against my attitude, so I let him take over while I take my much-needed break, still feeling a bit guilty."

As we begin evolving to a new self, we have to check with ourselves, notice what we're giving up and appreciate what we're gaining. This evolutionary process, which only begins in the second month, continues throughout the first year and the years beyond. It is important to know that this is a time of rapid psychological change for a woman, that she must undergo a significant degree of psychological dissolution—from her former self—and recomposition—to her evolving self!⁹ Therefore, it is not surprising that many women begin to have conflicting and ambivalent feelings about motherhood at this stage. We are just now truly beginning to realize that it means a *great* change for us, and we feel a little shaken by the whole process, uncertain whether we entirely want to go along.

What Are We Heading Toward?

There are always doubts, always enjoyable times and bad times, at each stage of our child's growth. This is inherent in being a parent despite whatever we might have thought before. So in certain ways, the ambivalences that we begin to experience in the second month are with us to stay; they never disappear entirely. What does change is that we become less bothered by them. The mother of a two-year-old can feel as frustrated with her child's behavior as the mother of a two-month-old. But by that time she knows and is familiar with the frustration and concern. She is not so upset by her feelings because she knows that it's all part of being a mother. Tomorrow her child will be a little charmer, and she will go through that day glowing, the frustration miles away. Earlier on, we don't know that, and so each new emotion takes on greater significance. We have not yet attained the flexibility of experience.

Basically, what begins around the second month is the pure taste of motherhood. It is new and unusual, and we have to taste it many times again before we accept it. We have to begin thinking about ourselves as different, not wholly different, but changed, nevertheless.

Most mothers do feel that parenthood is a maturing experience,[10] which in psychological terms means a process of expanding the personality through learning.[11] This learning process involves work, achievement, and creativity. No one would doubt that there is a great deal of learning, work, and creativity involved in being a parent, or that the personality is widened.

But we do, perhaps, express the new qualities of maturation in different ways. Many mothers feel a much greater sense of meaning or purpose to life. Suddenly it all makes sense—we have been given to, and now we give. Mothering can bring out new qualities of softness and affection in us. And the baby reminds us of the beauty of innocence and fresh perspectives. All of this greatly deepens and broadens our experience of life.

Most mothers say they wouldn't choose to return to their old selves after knowing these new dimensions, no matter how much they feel they have traded. And that is what we are heading toward—acceptance of ourselves as mothers and realistic understanding of the motherhood role, its drawbacks as well as its rewards. In learning this, we become new individuals, with a greater comprehension of life.

"I think I've matured. I am more responsive to other people's needs. I feel generally a more responsible person, socially speaking."

"Being a mother gives me a stake in the future. I'm now concerned about voting, air pollution, water and energy control. Becoming a mother has given me a greater sense of fulfillment."

"Giving birth was the most profound experience of my life thus far. I've never come closer to the true nature of human experience. Giving birth was not simply the act, it is experiencing a new life on a daily basis. It has made me substantially more patient and understanding and even a little better organized."

A Theory of Transitions

Psychologist William Bridges who has made a major study of transitions, emphasizes that we live in a production-line culture and that we have all inculcated that mentality.[12] We assume that our lives should fit the pattern of a "time for production or development," "time for functioning," and a "time for deterioration." The years roughly up to age twenty-one are for production, in which we should acquire all the parts and skills we need to function for the next forty years, before we become obsolete. If for some reason we seem to be still changing and "developing" during the supposed "functioning" years of our life, then we automatically assume that we are faulty in some way.

This mechanistic view denies the fact that people are constantly evolving throughout their lives, constantly learning what it means to be human. In fact, if that process of change stops, then there is a defect somewhere—and not the other way around. Though we are always learning, Bridges states, there are nevertheless times of rapid growth, and those are specifically around transition phases.

In looking at the way "passages" are handled in other cultures, Bridges observes certain patterns or rituals which help the person through the adjustment. The ritual usually involves a period of time when the person actually or symbolically goes into the wilderness to meditate on the changes. The introspection centers on two emotions—grief for what is being relinquished, the old self, and joy at what is coming, the maturity and further understanding of life.

Puberty is a typical such rite of passage, when childish ways and innocence are traded for secrets of the tribe and adulthood. Puberty is a time of conflicting emotions and often negativism. The person feels like neither a child nor an adult. The ceremony, the introspection, and time help in the transition to the next developmental stage.

When people return from the wilderness, it is expected that they are different and that they will be treated accordingly. It is assumed that the mourning period for the old self is almost finished and that the new self is recognized and accepted by the person. Often the person takes a new name to symbolize the change that has occurred.

The eddying of emotions in any transition is normal and powerful and it serves a purpose. There is hardly any life transition more profound than becoming a mother. Yet as this psychologist points out, transitional ceremonies, which are so helpful and necessary in other cultures, are nearly unknown or are perverted in ours. We are forced to do it alone.

Suggested reading:

Of Woman Born: Motherhood as Experience and Institution, by Adrienne Rich

The Mother Knot, by Jane Lazarre

Woman at Home, by Arlene Cardozo

Mothering: The Emotional Experience of Motherhood After Freud and Feminism, by Elaine Heffner

MONTHS 3 & 4

We will find as the year progresses that each stage in the baby's development toward being a more independent person and each stage in our corresponding adjustment to motherhood involve new challenges and new emotions. As we have noted, these emotions are often conflicting. More simply, being a mother means that we feel both positively and negatively toward the whole experience. One difference during the third and fourth month, though, is that we might feel both of these extremes to a much greater degree than before.

Big things begin to happen in the third and fourth months. Through smiling and grasping, the baby is beginning to seem more like a real person and more endearing than ever before. We feel very attached, reluctant to leave for fear we'll miss some charming moment, or that the baby will miss us and be disturbed.

Yet there are changes in us, too. We feel stronger, more capable. We are anxious to accomplish things again and to begin opening out our lives a little more. Fearing that we may never return to an acceptable position in our careers, or that we will never have time for outside pursuits, we become nearly obsessed with the desire to get into the mainstream again.

But worried feelings on leaving the baby with a sitter, or a relative inability to get much done for ourselves, makes us realize even more how much has changed in our lives. We may frequently feel bored with motherhood or resentful. Then we feel guilty for admitting to such supposedly inappropriate and unacceptable emotions.

But *all* of our feelings are justified and important. We have to begin accepting these and recognizing them as normal and necessary, if we are to take advantage of the crucial changes in ourselves.

Changes in the Baby and Our Responses

Those mothers who have not felt a true "love" for their babies prior to this time usually begin to do so now. Other mothers feel a deepening of their love and commitment to the child. A great deal of this response is because of slow but definite changes in the baby. The baby concentrates on faces now and relates through the eyes,[1] and smiles excitement at the attentions we give. The infant has turned a corner in starting to become a social being, and is as pleased by interactions with people as by having its physical needs met.

The baby coos, and we excitedly repeat these sounds. Given a full-faced toothless grin, we irresistibly smile back. The baby begins to reach for things, and we proudly present the rattle that has been dropped for so long because the baby didn't know it was capable of holding onto something. There are "conversations" and real "play periods" with the baby each day now, during which we feel an increasing closeness.

Our emotional connectedness and sensitivity are borne out by studies of maternal-child interaction at this age.

"The enmeshing of the infant's behavior with his mother's behavior becomes particularly clear when we study their interaction at a highly detailed, microscopic level," Rudolf Schaffer writes in *Mothering.* ". . . three-month-old infants and their mothers, looking at one another face to face, move their heads strikingly in time with one another. Film analysis reveals a pattern of mutual approach and withdrawal, according to which the infant turns his head away from his mother for a split second, mainly when she approaches him, and turns toward her as she withdraws from his visual field . . . We are rarely conscious of these patterns for they are so rapid that they can only be revealed by special techniques such as slowed down films. Their importance, as the basis of all direct social interaction, however, cannot be underestimated."[2]

We are the primary sources of sociability at this stage and also the main providers of stimulation. It is obvious now if it hadn't been earlier that the baby needs increasing and varying stimulation. If before it was sufficient to hold the baby or move the baby about when it seemed bored, now the child requires interesting things to look at that sparkle or move. Music is enjoyed, as are our monologues when changing diapers. If we go out for a walk, the baby strains to see what is around rather than being satisfied to be covered or held. The baby loves the free play of its arms and legs and occasionally discovers a flying hand that looks interesting to gnaw on. A drowsy baby at this age, if presented with an interesting object will remain awake for up to a half an hour in order to study it.[3]

It has been shown that babies "who are given early stimulation—who are rocked, carried, talked to, and smiled at—are less ir-ritable, have longer periods of concentration, develop a wider range of different responses and relate better to other people. The more they see, hear, and feel, the more they taste and smell, the more they get used to, the more they seek different experiences. In this way, early stimulation seems to foster greater learning."[4]

We instinctively seem to provide the sort of stimulation (or buffer to stimulation) that our babies need at any given time because of our sensitivity to them. We have placed ourselves in an empathetic position and have allowed ourselves to be paced by the baby's needs. We are now more casual about the baby's needs—that is, we don't worry about them as much as we did before—we can devote more time to the developing needs for stimulation and sociability. This is a fresh and exciting new phase for us. It's fun to be able to give to the baby in new ways and to see our gifts so enthusiastically received.

This is not to suggest, however, that the baby is any less demanding or much easier to deal with. The unexplainable crying at certain hours of the day might persist. The baby might have trad-ed one reason for fussiness for another. Or any number of other new and incomprehensible problems might have arisen. But in a good mood, the baby is genuinely appealing because of this newly developed sociability, and that is the welcome change.

Grow Faster!

The baby's first major step into the realm of increased awareness and responsiveness causes us to get greedy. All of a sudden we are more eager than ever for the next stage! The charts say the baby should be able to sit up in a couple of months; and thinking about what that new, independent position would bring both of us—new perspectives, new delights—we are impatient.

We are sure every cranky day is the harbinger of a first tooth. Daily, we hopefully sit up the baby, then watch it sag.

There are probably two sources for this feeling. One, as in pregnancy, we just can't wait to see what this marvelous individual is going to be like. And two, we desire more freedom for ourselves. Our fantasies about each approaching stage involve the baby being less demanding. But while each new stage helps us to see more of the baby's personality, it doesn't actually free us much more. There are always new and different demands.

Really, we should take the advice of all the grandmothers and aunts who ever lived and try to fully enjoy each stage, because the baby won't be in it very long!

Changes in Us

By month three or four, the baby is usually sleeping somewhat more predictably so we are not so tired. We are increasingly able to do the grocery shopping, laundry, and cooking. Even the housework is getting organized and done on a more regular basis. The plants are no longer dying at the rate of two a week. In short, we are starting to gain more control over the details of our new life. As we're able to fulfill more of these daily tasks, both confidence and sense of self-acceptance increases: we're finally beginning to feel the way we *thought* we'd feel three weeks after the birth. Even some of the extra weight we gained seems to be slipping away.

We probably feel ready to take on a bit more, to accomplish a few things other than handling immediate family needs. We are itching to get involved in something for ourselves. This feeling is usually in combination with a fear that we'll never get involved again in anything unless we do it *now.* Although we've been relatively isolated and focused on the baby for three or four months (not actually a very long time), it feels like an eternity because so much has happened and changed in that time. We feel that we've been "out of it" for a year or two and want to make up for lost time.

If we haven't done so already, we slowly work up the courage to leave the baby for an evening or an afternoon or longer, arguing to ourselves that we'll appreciate the child even more when we return. As frightening as it can be to leave the baby with someone else, we decide we really need to do it. Our frustration is building—or it may be a matter of necessity.

We take the plunge and interview a babysitter, only to find that we have trouble judging how good someone is with children. Nevertheless, we finally set up the time to leave, trying to mesh it, at least the first time, with when the baby will be sleeping, so our absence won't be noticed; and we go.

It's hard, nearly impossible to do that first time. We force ourselves to walk away, feeling light because of not carrying all the paraphernalia, but also anxious. We call after an hour, and probably return home early. Even though the baby is happy and the babysitter looks confident, we feel that there is a lie being perpetrated here, that the baby cried miserably the whole time. But it is a pleasant surprise to find that we can actually leave and that disaster will not befall the baby or mother.

It gets easier each time. Even though we could hardly think of anything else but returning home at first, each time we are gradually able to concentrate more on whatever is before us. We gratefully find that it's refreshing and necessary to be able to leave now and then.

But as we start to venture away from the baby, we realize how closely we are tied. This brings us face-to-face once again with what mothering means. We are tethered not so much by a sense of responsibility as by a feeling that we are needed, that we love the baby desperately. And yet we may feel restricted, too.

Just when we're finally strong and confident enough to begin to test our wings as individuals there is the sudden recognition that we have a string tied to one leg and cannot fly far from the nest. Dismay can set in once again, similar to what we might have experienced earlier. Now we might not feel stuck quite as much, since we know that we can and do leave the baby, but a deeper realization seems to be dawning: about what we've given up and about our own and society's expectations.

"I am extremely concerned, in fact frightened, about suspending my career. I've heard too many stories and seen too many women whose self-confidence faded when they ceased to work. Later, they appeared to have lost the sense that they could function and be competent in the working world. It can be a vicious circle with others, expecially their husbands, losing respect for them.

"I'm afraid, when all I have to talk about when my husband comes home is trivia. I'm afraid when I see the continuous progression of my profession and know I'm not keeping up. I'm afraid when my day is spent with cleaning up, laundry, cooking, bill-paying, and shopping. I have nothing, it seems, to show for my time that is lasting except my son. I'm afraid, because someday my son won't need my full-time attention either."

"I became involved in other activities when Britte was about two months old. Part of discovering a new inward side of me has been augmented by my yoga practice and study. I attend classes on an ongoing, intensive basis. It has fulfilled my needs to be around other people, to do something physical, and to remove myself from the house for a while. It also gives Mick and Britte time without me around. When I first started leaving Britte, I would think of her and my milk would let down! Having adjusted to that, it wasn't too hard because she was usually with Mick, and I think their time together was valuable."

Self-Expectations and Self Doubts

"Many women come to motherhood completely unaware of its drawbacks. And when they discover them, they often feel they are lacking as mothers if they somehow do not relish all the negatives, since a cardinal part of the motherhood myth is that *liking* being a mother is a must if you are to *be* a good mother."[5]

There are good days and bad days. There are days when we have more energy and patience; there are days when we have less. There are times when the baby is responsive and doing something new and easy to handle; there are times when the baby is cranky, dissatisfied, and dull.

Our expectation is that we should be fairly consistently content with being a mother, and that we can provide the best mothering under those circumstances. We are disappointed in ourselves when some days we dislike motherhood, and we may genuinely doubt our ability to be good mothers because of these fluctuations in attitude.

In reality, no one is content with any job day-in and day-out. There are bad, stressful, demanding days when things go wrong, when we loathe the job and the quality of our work. Relationships are not blissfully calm and serene all the time either. There are greater and lesser degrees of involvement and intensity with the other person. There are struggles and arguments and bad feelings as well as good. And yet, we expect so much more of ourselves as mothers. We expect the impossible. Then we blame ourselves for not measuring up.

We assume, that because we don't always like being a mother, we must be a bad one. *All* mothers dislike motherhood off and on. That's normal. And especially in the first year, when we're just coming to terms with the life of a mother, we tend to feel the negative—as well as the positive—sides more powerfully. As we're inexperienced with these emotions, they can frighten and worry us. And since mothers are never supposed to feel negative or doubtful or bored, we don't talk about the feelings, and then they fester.

A book which realistically describes the feelings inherent in motherhood and suggests a helpful way to deal with them is *Mothering: The Emotional Experience of Motherhood after Freud and Feminism,* by Elaine Heffner. The author is a psychiatrist who works with mothers and young children. She says, "Mothers are not prepared for the kinds of negative feelings they will have toward their children. They are not helped to understand that such feelings are usual and normal. It is typical for anger to be aroused by the stress of child care and the behavior of children. The first few years of child rearing are physically taxing, with long work hours and not enough sleep, repetitive tasks, and deprivation of adult company and mental stimulation."[6]

Yet one reason we are afraid to voice these feelings, she says, is that since Freud there has been a "tendency to measure success in mothering in terms of the child's mental health. . . ."[7]

"Emotional adjustment has been interpreted to mean perfection, both for the child and for the mother," Dr. Heffner writes. "Mental health, happiness, absence of frustration, freedom from pain, all these join together in the mother's mind. To be successful she believes she must dissolve negative feelings and find no evidence of pain or conflict. Mothers have not been taught that problems are in the nature of things. Life includes frustration, pain, conflict, and anger. Child rearing includes helping children master and deal appropriately with these feelings. In order to master feelings, one must feel them. How can a mother help her child if she has come to believe her own success rests on finding no evidence of such feelings or behavior? If her definition of good mothering is the avoidance of problems, the child's expression of his feelings then becomes an assault on her, a reproach. Anything that seems negative arouses her anxiety."[8]

A mother, she states, "should not be misled by her wish to be omnipotent, all-powerful, all-giving, the perfect mother, who will right all the wrongs of her own childhood. She is simply an imperfect human being with needs of her own."[9]

"I remember one day finally admitting to myself that I was bored and immediately retreating from the idea. It was like confessing to hating my child. I never told any one about it for months."

One job of a mother is to help a child understand that his or her own feelings are not wrong, whatever they may be. "To achieve this objective," Dr. Heffner explains, "a mother must begin with the assurance that she has the right to her own feelings and needs. She has a right *not* to sacrifice herself for her child. She has a right to feel anger, frustration, hate, rejection, the need to depend on some-one herself. None of these makes her a bad mother. In the same way, the child's demands, dependency, need for care, aggressive and angry feelings do not make him a bad child."[10]

Boredom and Resentments

Boredom is one typical "negative" emotion that all mothers feel, but that we condemn ourselves for feeling. There are long hours in-volved in mothering. Not just that it's a twenty-four-hour-a-day, 365-day-a-year responsibility, which is enough in itself, but that each actual hour that the baby is awake lasts a long time. (It is an unusual baby who will quietly entertain itself for much longer than half an hour at a stretch.)

Whether we're at home shaking a rattle or in the park point-ing out the ducks, those activities don't hold *our* attention for very long, and no matter how creative we are, we simply run out of ideas of things to do after a while. We wish we could just go somewhere and read or sew or do something on our level for a change. We look at the clock and it's 2 P.M. Four more hours before the ritual of bath and bed. We yawn at the thought of all those hours to fill.

Some days we work up to a fever pitch creating a new toy or mobile, something that we're sure will fascinate the baby for hours.

That keeps us occupied, and we feel so motherly and inventive. But after two days the baby doesn't even glance at it, and we can't think of anything else to make. We long for the day when the baby will stack blocks or look at books.

Some of this boredom is due to the plain fact that at this age there is *not* much intellectual challenge or enough change to keep us intrigued and the daily tasks required of us are relatively simple, but time-consuming. Studies suggest that women with more education or with professional working experience actually do have a harder time adjusting to the tasks of motherhood than other women do.[11] These women are used to a faster pace and diversified challenges. There are some interesting perspectives about life and ourselves we can learn, we freely admit, but the day-to-day work is often dull.

One woman psychologist, writing about the transition to parenthood, suggests that for some women "the personal outcome of experience in the parent role is not a higher level of maturation, but the negative outcome of a depressed sense of self-worth, if not actual personality deterioration. There is considerable evidence that this is more prevalent than we recognize." She also states that women "lose ground in personal development and self-esteem during the early and middle years of adulthood, whereas men gain ground in these respects during the same years."[12]

Maybe, as this psychologist suggests, some of us do actually lose ground in our early mothering years, permanently to be hindered by feelings of professional and personal inadequacy. And maybe we don't. But in either case, we have been taught that whatever the price, we are fulfilling a higher destiny. However, there is a clever contradiction here that we become aware of on our blacker days. In general, mothers are respected, but women are viewed contemptuously by society: a mother is performing a "glorious" task, but let's leave it to the women to do.

At this point boredom turns into resentment, a second common but "negative" or "inappropriate" emotion. The prime target of resentment is the husband, of course, who symbolizes all of male society. He, being a man, we mutter, simply and happily walks away from his family and is involved in something different each day, while we sit twiddling our thumbs and cleaning dirty diapers. Why, just because we carried and delivered the child, are we also relegated to the mental status of a child? Yes, of course, we chose to be where we are, and when you come right down to it, we want to be here most of the time. But we never expected it to be like this and we feel slightly used, by our husbands and society.

This feeling can be a deeper, more pervasive resentment than we might have experienced before. Earlier we might have been afraid to admit such a negative emotion to our repertoire of postpartum feelings. But now it might have grown and is with us part of nearly every day. It might be adversely affecting our openness and affection with our husbands, and causing a brooding mild depression that just seems to be a basic part of life.

> *"My husband goes off to work in the morning and returns at night. I've always expected if I'm not working to take care of the daily grind—the laundry, cleaning, and cooking. I remember what it was like to come home after a full day of work, to be hungry and tired—so I try to have dinner ready. Lately though, I've been feeling what a treat it must be to have everything so different during the day. To have projects to be working on without the interruptions of your baby fussing and to be involved with other people.*
>
> *"I don't resent my husband, I resent his leaving his clothes lying around or his breakfast dishes, dirty and sitting out. I resent what seems to me to be this attitude of 'you're home all day and I'm working hard.' I resent being on duty twenty-four hours a day with the baby. Still, I feel I've made my choices, and I can still make choices which might help me get through this time."*

"One thing I am aware of is that my baby and I are both females. I get edgy whenever my husband infers that we are on the same level. For example, I don't like it when he doles out the same and equal affections to both of us. I don't want to compete with my little girl for my husband's attention."

There are two choices at this point. Either we free up more time for our own pursuits, perhaps going back to work; or we begin to value ourselves more as mothers, accepting the range of our emotions and working to make each day stimulating for ourselves as well as for the baby.

More time alone or going back to work will do wonders for flagging self-esteem almost immediately, as we begin to feel valuable as more than "just" a mother. If we go the other route, remaining at home, it is imperative that we begin to reject society's values that we've internalized—that mothers are both glorious and worthless. We need to begin understanding that motherhood has negative as well as positive sides and to accept *all* of our feelings.

It should be just as easy, for instance, to say that it was a boring day as that it was a good one and not feel uneasy about it. More experienced mothers talk about their boredom and frustrations without a second thought. They know that those feelings are only part of the whole experience and that they are not anything to be ashamed of. To admit the extent of the "bad" feelings frees us to enjoy the "good" ones even more.

As for the actual problem of what to do each day, we have to put our creative talents to work thinking of things we'd enjoy doing and ways that we could manage to take the baby along. At this age, the baby is pretty portable, and we can go quite a few places with her: museums, stores, library, hiking.

We are still aware of those things we cannot do, of course, but if we've decided that the baby is the highest priority for the time being, then there is satisfaction just in knowing that we're sticking to what is an important decision for us.

Arlene Cardozo in her book, *Woman at Home* points out that women, in desiring to follow the men's lead, have accepted the notion that work outside the home is the most fulfilling, and significant work. All too frequently, in fact, jobs are stressful, competitive, and enhance the belief that in order to be a worthwhile person we have to be upwardly mobile and ambitious. If instead of choosing those priorities, we choose to develop close warm, human relationships, to follow creative pursuits, or simply slow down to appreciate each day and season, then being at home is the better, more "liberating" choice.[13]

If we start to respect what we're doing—and our reasons for doing it—self-confidence and esteem will grow. But we have to sort out *exactly* what we want and need most of all and then pursue it accepting whatever attendant feelings may come, too.

> *"I was little leery at first about suspending my career. To feel safe I decided to enter graduate school so as to stay in touch with it. As my pregnancy developed, and then more so after my daughter's birth, I noticed a change in my self-awareness. Knowing and securing a place and identification within the society became less important. Instead of trying to see who I was among them, I went inside to discover who I was . . . And I'm still young enough to be a player in the game later on, if I elect to do so."*

Suggested Reading:

The Mother Knot, by Jane Lazarre

Woman at Home, by Arlene Cardozo

Mothering: The Emotional Experience of Motherhood After Freud and Feminism, by Elaine Heffner

Of Woman Born: Motherhood as Experience and Institution, by Adrienne Rich

CHAPTER SEVEN

MONTHS 5 & 6 AND WORKING MOTHERS

The baby, suddenly blossoming in what she or he can do, is gearing up for the great leaps in social and motor development that will be made in the second half of the first year. Through being able to reach for and grasp things and being able to sit up with perhaps only a little support, the baby has made the first step toward actively pursuing its curiosities. The world, from this new perspective, is so fascinating that less of our attention might be required as the child explores with eyes and mouth the toys that we have provided.

This first little sign of independence combined with a fairly common "lag" in breast-feeding interest at this stage makes us feel confident about our successful nurturing to this point. We have clearly gotten over the major early hurdles and might feel as though we could go on having children forever—if they would all turn out like this one! We begin to consider weaning, in response to the apparent disinterest; and because things have calmed down so much, it is a time that we might think about returning to work.

Naturally some women return to work within a couple of weeks of the birth, some within a few months, some not for years. But, it seems that mothers who decided to take an indeterminate time off from work first begin seriously considering a return at about this stage. They have attained a certain degree of self-confidence about mothering and are, at the same time, feeling the need for something more. There may also be the feeling that their babies need them less now. Whenever mothers go back to work, whether immediately or after months or years, they often face similar problems and worries, as well as gaining new pleasures. These common issues are presented here.

What's the Baby Doing?

The baby is laughing and alert and literally sitting up to take notice. She is responsive, in a fairly good mood most of the time, and even may be sleeping through the night. Games of peek-a-boo or tickling elicit squeals of delight. The baby will study and mouth the rattle, throw objects and pick them up again, just to see how they work. Though our company is preferred, the baby is also happy alone for short periods, given enough stimulation close by.

The baby seems to love people, especially children. Everyone appears to offer something new and intriguing, but it's clear that children offer special enticements, that in them the baby recognizes a unique link to himself/herself. Children know just the right antics to amuse the baby simply by being themselves. We're surprised at and pleased for this clever awareness and sociability in the baby.

The baby is so curious and happy much of the time that this behavior is infectious. Playtimes with mother and baby or family times are beginning to be a lot of fun. The baby offers the bodily excitement of pumping its arms up and down and giggles joyously as proof of the pleasure taken in our company; and we find ourselves equally excited. There is no doubt that the baby is changing rapidly, becoming more sociable, and gaining motor skills that will lead to more independence.

We remain, of course, the most important person in the baby's life, and though we are starting to receive some very definite rewards from being in that position, still the burden of responsibility is great. The hours are long, and increasingly for some of us, the challenge is not how to accomplish all the many and varied chores to be done each day, but rather, how to get through the day with equanimity. If flagging self-esteem is dragging us down, returning to work looks more and more appealing.

Combining Work and Motherhood

Many thorny questions arise when we consider going back to work, partly because of the deep emotions involved and partly because of the complex logistics. We have not only to consider ourselves and a work arrangement, but we also have to think about what working will mean for the baby, husband, and the household responsibilities we've assumed.

By far the person we're most concerned about is the baby. What effect will a daily separation have? The prevailing assumption for the last twenty or thirty years has been that such separations have grave and long-lasting effects on young children. Pediatricians, parental advisers, and society in general have all followed suit in advising mothers to remain at home for the crucial first few years—at least.

However, the basis for that assumption is two-fold. First, the children for whom there were grave effects because of parental separation were institutionalized children deprived of their parents because of the worst conditions—war and being refugees. Second, since Freud it has been assumed that the first two years are the most significant years for healthy emotional development. Now that purely theoretical assumption is being questioned, and the tentative results seem to indicate that, while important, the first two years are probably not much more critical than any other of the years of childhood.[1]

A study conducted by Boston pediatrician Dr. Mary Howell in 1973, and widely noted since then, showed that there were "no uniformly harmful effects on family life or on the growth and development of children"[2] when the mother worked outside the home. Further, she found that:

"Professional child caretakers observe that approximately six hours per day is the maximum amount of time most interested and able adults can invest in meaningful interaction with children. Full-time homemaker-mothers report that they spend, on the average, six-plus hours in child care, when they have more than one child, compared to employed mothers who spend four-plus hours in child care. It has been estimated that the difference in 'attentive' care is probably not significant."[3]

When we are home there are always other demands and other things we want to do for stimulation so that the meaningful time spent with our children may actually be less than we think. We might spend a lot of time with the baby, but it is not always quality time. Those of us who are working mothers, on the other hand, being away from our babies for a big part of the day, are anxious to relate to them in important ways when we come home.

"I had thought that I would do my writing as the baby slept. I was wrong; he rarely napped. I was frustrated, because I had decided that I should have him with me all the time during the first couple of

*years. Finally, near the end of the first year I knew I
wasn't being a good mother any more. I sent him to a
babysitter who took in other small children every morning. The response was amazing.*

*"He loved playing with people his own age and
came home happy and tired. I suddenly stopped
resenting him because I had at least a half a day to
myself. We spent lovely, chummy afternoons together,
really appreciating each other. And he seems to
understand and like the fact that I have something else
in my life besides him. One of his favorite games is to
sit at my desk and pretend to write."*

Not only do working mothers often offer their children more
when they are actually with them, but those mothers also report
that their working sometimes seems to have other positive side effects for their children. Some feel that their children are more
sociable, since they relate to at least one other person outside the
family. And others feel that their regular comings and goings to
work each day promote a feeling of trust in their children; though
mother goes away, she always returns at a certain time.[4]

Aside from the fear of psychologically damaging our babies,
we also worry that the babysitter will replace us in our children's
affections, or that we'll miss much of their childhood. Experienced
working mothers are quick to point out that the babysitter might
have the children eight hours a day, but the family has them all the
rest of the time, mornings, evenings, weekends, vacations. And
babysitters add that kids never confuse mother with anyone else.

The question of *when* in our children's lives to return to work
can be a crucial factor in both their and our successful adjustments.
Many women feel that after two years their children should be well
enough established to cope with mother being away for the day.
Age two has been the magic number because of that assumption
about the first two years being so important. However, mothers
report that trying to leave a two-year-old is like trying to wrench

yourself free from an ardent lover. Two-year-olds are too aware. They've come to expect and require the mother's presence, and are very upset by changes in her schedule. It is probably easier in early infancy, when the baby is still adaptable and can "grow into" the situation, and knows nothing else but that mother leaves for a part of each day and returns later.

Another important ingredient in returning to work is finding good child care. For a first-time mother the task can be quite intimidating. Often we haven't decided whether we want a babysitter at home or if we want to take the baby out somewhere, which is the first part of the decision. And always we are shocked at the cost of whatever arrangement we decide on. But the importance of the child-care arrangements in successfully going back to work cannot be overemphasized.

Feeling good about the child care and the timing of the return to work, knowing that our children will not be harmed by our leaving them can make the psychological adjustment for us much easier. But when we return to work we probably have as much adjusting in store for us as our children do.

We will be fulfilling two careers, that of mother and working woman. Unlike our husbands, and contrary to our liberated expectations, we are very much the dominant parent who feels responsible for child care and for problems with the baby when things don't seem to be going well. Both careers are important to us. But the underlying assumption is that we would foresake work for the baby if it came to that. We walk a tightrope of loving our outside involvement and loving our baby, and hoping that neither adversely affects the other. Many women do feel that if a mother is truly convinced that career and baby can enhance each other, then the adjustment is much easier.

"I find having a child trememdously helpful to
my creative abilities. His being gives me more energy,
more spontaneity, and more joie de vivre. *Also, due to*

his presence, I am forced to discipline myself in my
work which I really need and like."

There is a tremendous amount of work involved. Working mothers cannot simply come home and relax, there are then family responsibilities. And we frequently feel overworked, tired, and stressed. On the other hand, we may find that the complementing jobs energize us. Going from one to the other is refreshing on an emotional level, if somewhat exhausting physically.

Our lives do seem to become further restricted though, narrowing down to the essentials of work, family time, couple time, and household responsibility time. There simply isn't much time or energy left after that.

On an emotional level, working mothers are often saddled with guilt, no matter how well chosen their day care is, and no matter how rewarding their jobs are. Society (and sometimes nonworking mothers) still deprecate the working mother who has very young children at home. She is considered unfeeling and unmotherly. At the same time, she has internalized enough of this attitude to fear it in herself, too. If her children start to have problems, her first thought is that it is because she is working. "Much of the psychological stress working mothers have to deal with comes from their perpetual effort to bolster their own convictions. Often the only support they find for their convictions and way of life comes from other working mothers," Jean Curtis has found.[5]

But there are a lot of advantages involved, too. Leading a life separate from the one we lead at home can be intoxicatingly refreshing. To enjoy adult relationships and challenges, to feel needed and important for our special skills, and simply to have an independent life are all factors that add to a sense of worth. It could well be that working mothers, who feel better about themselves more of the time than non-working mothers do, can offer a more positive environment to their children by having the children know that when the mother is at home she is happily at home and wants very much to be with them.

In Sum

According to the Labor Department, in 1975 51% of the mothers of preschoolers worked full-time outside the home. There are many reasons for this, including economic necessity and changing values that allow women to pursue their own interests and needs more than in the past. We each have our own specific reasons and make our own particular arrangements if we work outside the home. And despite the inevitable struggles and hardships, most working women feel that their outside work is necessary and enhancing for them.

For the other half of us who choose to remain at home, the plateau the baby has reached around six months, allows us a sort of breathing space between the earlier primarily physical problems we faced and the more emotional challenges that will arise in the next few months. The baby is friendly, and we feel more relaxed. Motherhood, and being at home we might feel, are settling gracefully upon us.

Suggested Reading:

Working Mothers, by Jean Curtis

CHAPTER EIGHT

MONTHS 7 & 8

The baby is clearly attached to the significant people in its life, so that now as the baby is beginning to be able to creep or crawl away, the reassurance of having a loved one to come back to is also needed. Strangers may be frightening, and the baby clings in frantic embraces if they approach too quickly or come too close. It is intensely gratifying to know that we are so special; and the baby's new antics of beginning to explore alone a little bit are wonderful to watch.

There are, of course, new demands on us, but we are starting to take these changes in stride. We might feel nervous or frustrated on certain days and have certain problems, but we are no longer devastated by them. We know the situation will evolve and that we just have to make the best of whatever is occurring at the time.

Many women at this stage begin to have a broader awareness of what the social and lifestyle implications are of having a child. More and more of their friends and social activities involve people with children than before. And the fact that there is little private time for either parent is an accepted reality now.

Fortunately, while many of these changes are still noted and perhaps even discussed, they do not seem to take on immense, painful proportions. The baby is beginning to seem like plenty of reward for what has been given up. Another way of putting it is that we are more accepting of the fact that we are in what has been called the "generative phase" of life—when we obtain our gratification more from giving to others rather than from concentrating on ourselves.

Developments in the Baby and Our Reciprocal Responses

Around seven or eight months the baby starts to demand more of our physical presence for emotional reassurance. As the baby begins to realize that it really is separate from us, the world is suddenly both exciting and frightening. The baby can move away from us, if it desires, to handle and mouth some intriguing new object. For the first time, the baby can focus both its attention and movements on something other than what we have offered, and that is an astounding new revelation. But at the same time, the distance that the baby can put between itself and us can seem enormous. The baby is not sure it actually wanted to be so far away and screams out of frustration and worry.

Meanwhile, glad about this relative independence, we might have withdrawn somewhat, thinking that was needed to consolidate the baby's new-found autonomy, and also because we were eager to be doing other things. But our absence or emotional withdrawal is found intolerable by the baby and only increases the worry and screaming. The baby requires both independence and our continued involvement. We are needed nearby so the baby can "check in"with us now and then.

Babies at this stage are also capable of multiple attachments to people they see frequently and like. Mother and father and maybe grandparents or special friends are all thrilled to be recognized and so accepted. Babies begin now to see themselves as distinct and to see other people as different from each other, too. While this seems to prompt a delightful burgeoning in sociability, it also causes fear of those people who are not among the "special" ones.

There is no doubt that this is a critical time in a child's development. The initial bond of trust that has been growing in the early months is put to the test at this point for the first time and the baby needs to know that the mother or other significant people are still available whenever needed, even though they may not be needed all the time. Babies need to know that they have some haven of security and familiarity when they are suddenly perceiving so many new things.

These problems are not physical ones, they are almost entirely emotional; and this is perhaps the first time we've confronted the fact that the baby needs us on many levels. Development is proceeding on many fronts at the same time: as much as we have to protect the baby now from swallowing a stray pin on the floor that suddenly can be reached, we have to be concerned about budding fears and loves and feelings of insecurity.

We might at first wonder: Are we giving enough love? Maybe we did not establish trust very well, since the baby so easily becomes distressed if we just leave the room for an instant. Is the baby going to be scarred for life if we absolutely have to go out for a long period and leave a sitter in charge? Life had been so easy recently; we had been feeling so confident, and now this. Are we doing something wrong?

Many mothers also feel irritated at this behavior in the baby. The constant clinginess and fussiness can wear the patience; and it seems so unecessary, since only a week ago everyone was the baby's friend and she or he could play happily alone for short periods. It seems as if the child has taken a step backwards, toward being more like a little baby rather than toward growing up. We had, perhaps, been used to times of relative freedom, and now our total attention is required. We're not accustomed to that any more, and it seems like an unreasonable demand. In addition, if we've become able to admit our negative feelings, we definitely can say that this is a frustrating stage and we don't like it. This may cause us to worry that we will not do the right thing for the baby during this stage.

Nevertheless, most of us intuitively seem to handle ourselves as we should for our babies' benefit. As in other situations in early mothering, we respond sometimes without completely understanding the source of the baby's difficulty. We reassure the baby, give automatically, and with pleasure, whatever seems to be needed.

And, in fact, the baby *is* irresistible often now. The clean, honest facial expressions that belie exactly what is felt are disarming. The glee and uncomplicated excitement about new objects or sights is infectious. Proud of such accomplishments as standing while holding onto something or taking those first few crawling paces, the baby beams triumph at us, and we fall in love all over again. We take it for granted that the baby seems so much a real person now who laughs and explores and possesses real determination. Sometimes we are shocked to remember how small and incapable the same child was only a few months ago.

This is all part of the normal developmental pattern, challenges to which we adjust. Joy as well as ambivalences and worries are natural on our part. We will be off-balance for a short time as we reorient ourselves around new demands, but soon everything will fall into place and we will have gained more experience and confidence about our mothering.

Lifestyle Changes

Around this time, because of the baby's new mobility and increased demands, and maybe because we've simply been mothers long enough to see the patterns, we observe that some permanent changes have occurred in our lifestyles.

Our social relationships might have dwindled down to just a few close friends. We seem to do less entertaining and less initiating of new relationships. The exception to that is that we have been drawn to other young parents and have begun socializing with them on a limited basis.

But it is often difficult to find times that are compatible for both families. Schedules vary and the children's needs intrude, so that the relationships we develop with other parents don't always feel as satisfying as the ones we had before there were children in the picture.

And yet there are difficulties with the old friendships too, particularly if the other people don't have children. Either they don't understand that flexibility with a child's schedule is not always feasible and grumble about how we've lost our spontaneity—which might be partially true for the time being. Or they might carry on as if nothing had changed, trying to maintain conversations over the baby's screams and ignoring the fact that we are too distracted trying to soothe the baby to pay attention to them. Sometimes the biggest difference between us and our childless friends is that they do not understand the profound experience we are going through. Words alone cannot express the emotions and changes that we feel, and so suddenly, there can be a barrier (of varying proportions) between us and our old friends. In many respects, they represent aspects of our old lives.

There is often at this stage a logistical problem, too, that hinders socializing. If before we could simply take our babies along and put them quietly to bed in a back room at the appropriate time, we begin to find now that they are not so cooperative along those lines any more. The physical task of dealing with a tired, fussing baby who refuses to go to sleep in new surroundings is anything but conducive to relaxed, pleasant social interactions.

Increasingly, because it's easy and satisfying, we tend to spend time at home as a family instead of seeking a lot of outside connections. Given that social relationships are at times more frustrating than they are worth—and that the family is fulfilling more of our social needs—we might welcome this change.

Another change we might notice more at this point is in our former entertainment or recreational pursuits. Hiking, camping, skiing, boating, and any other number of outdoor activities can be done with a baby, but there is a difference. They are harder to do, and this tends to reduce the pleasures.

Late night dancing, concerts, and just jumping into the car to catch an old "flick" across town have diminished or disappeared altogether from our lives. Then there is the perfectly planned evening, with expensive theater tickets and babysitter lined up, dashed when the baby suddenly develops a high temperature.

When the baby is seven- or eight-months-old, we begin to realize that these are going to be long-term changes in our lives. If before we assumed that we were curtailing our activities just while the baby was so vulnerable, now we recognize that there are always going to be ways that the baby will influence our activities. No longer so vulnerable, the baby is more alert and needs a fairly consistent daily routine. Familiar settings are more comfortable. Two months from now babies might not be as particular about where they are, but then they'll be able to move around so quickly that we'll find it easier to have them only in relatively safe places. Unless we leave the baby behind for the three days we go backpacking or unless we can work out some alternate plan for care in the mornings after we've been up late the night before, we will tend to indulge in fewer of those old activities.

"We can't be as spontaneous as before. We still can go on a lot of outings, but they have to be much more carefully planned."

"Most of the changes in our lifestyle have probably been for the better. I feel I must take care of myself both physically and emotionally as I have someone who depends on me for virtually everything. However, the house is always a mess, it seems, and periods of uninterrupted concentration are hard to come by."

Another major difference felt by both parents is much less individual time alone. There is work time and family or couple time, all of which are necessary. But there is little time left for the separate individual activities that were a big part of life before. We as mothers probably adjust to this fact faster, because we have to. But fathers tend to think for a longer period that things will eventually get back to "normal." They feel frustrated at being pulled in so many directions. We nod our heads knowingly when they complain about something we have faced daily for months.

"The main thing is that although I have a lot of free time, it seems like I cannot count on long periods of uninterrupted time to really concentrate on something. Even when the baby is not demanding my full attention, just her presence makes it difficult to do anything really serious."

"Although Michael agreed to tend our baby in the evenings when he came home, often his way of tending seemed to be to ignore her. It just drove me bats."

Everyone experiences the adjustment to the lifestyle changes differently. Many women simply accept the facts; they feel a sort of loss, but willingly trade the old pleasures for the new family ones.

Other women find giving up the old patterns one of the hardest parts of maternal adjustments. They never expected that such major changes would be required of them.

The Generative Phase

Adult development is a popular topic nowadays, focusing our attention on the fact that adults continue to evolve and grow just as children do; and that as with childhood growth, different stages can be delineated. Erik Erikson in the late 1950s sketched out a growth chart for human beings that has since become well known and accepted. He called it the "Eight Stages of Man." The first five stages concern childhood and youth; the last three are the stages of adulthood. As it is sometimes interesting to look at our lives from a broader viewpoint, representing the experiences of many human beings, I will apply Erikson's theory to the adjustments of parenthood.

Erikson is concerned with the growth of the healthy individual identity. Identity is, of course, that sense of ourselves as being distinct from anyone else and being unique and valuable. Each stage of development, he believes, gives us greater understanding of our personal identities and leads us on to a consolidation and acceptance of ourselves.

The first stage of adulthood he describes as "Intimacy versus Isolation:"

"When childhood and youth come to an end, life, so the saying goes, begins, by which we mean work or study for a specified career, sociability with the other sex, and in time, marriage and a family of one's own. But it is only after a reasonable sense of identity has been established that real intimacy with the other sex (or, for that matter, with any other person or even with oneself) is possible. . . . The youth who is not sure of his identity shies away from interpersonal intimacy; but the surer he becomes of himself, the more he seeks it in the form of friendship, combat, leadership, love, and inspiration."[1]

So the task of this first stage is to become sure enough of oneself to establish intimate relationships with other people or with another person.

Erickson's second stage centers on "Generativity versus Self-Absorption or Stagnation:"

"Generativity is primarily the interest in establishing and guiding the next generation. . . . The principal thing to realize is that this is a stage of the growth of the healthy personality and that where such enrichment fails altogether, regression from generativity to an obsessive need for pseudo-intimacy takes place, often with a pervading sense of stagnation and interpersonal impoverishment. Individuals who do not develop generativity often begin to indulge themselves as if they were their own one and only child."[2]

Erikson points out that even though "there are people who, from misfortune or because of special and genuine gifts in other directions, do not apply this drive to offspring," still they fulfill "their kind of parental responsibility" by devoting themselves "to other forms of altruistic concern and creativity."[3] It seems essential to the human maturational process that we finally and purposefully direct our attentions and efforts outside ourselves, taking as our primary concern the welfare of others. Only in that objective way, Erikson implies, can we fully understand our specific individual characteristics and our common humanity.

The final stage is designated "Integrity versus Despair and Disgust."

"Only he who in some way has taken care of things and people and has adapted himself to the triumphs and disappointments of being, by necessity, the originator of others and the generator of things and ideas—only he may gradually grow the fruit of the seven stages. I know no better word for it than integrity. Lacking a clear definition, I shall point to a few attributes of this stage of mind. It is the acceptance of one's own and only life cycle and of the people who have become significant to it as something that had to be and that, by necessity, permitted of no substitutions. It thus means a new, different love of one's parents, free of the wish that they should have been different, and an acceptance of the fact that one's life is one's own responsibility. It is a sense of comradeship with men and women of distant times and of different pursuits, who have created order and objects and sayings conveying human dignity and love. . . ."[4]

To carry his ideas into a discussion about parenthood as part of the life cycle, we can see that Erikson believes each stage must be successfully traversed before one can proceed to the next stage. In his eyes, generativity or parenthood is an essential step along the way to personal integrity and to an understanding of human nature and dignity.

The withdrawal of attention from our own self-absorption and the focussing of our concern in parental responsibility is at the base of our struggle at about the seventh and eighth months of the baby's life. We genuinely wish at times that this wasn't required of us, that we could indulge ourselves again and not have to worry about anyone else's needs. But at the same time, we are beginning to respect this new giving side of ourselves, and the baby is rewarding us in many fresh and exciting ways. We are groping toward our own personal sense of integrity and acceptance.

> *"I never knew I was capable of such giving and love."*

> *"I'd love to just go out and stay out all night dancing, or go away on a romantic weekend, but it's not really possible. The main way having a child has matured me is that there is now someone I am really responsible for and who depends on me. My husband depends on me too but not in the same way, and I also don't feel responsible for him in this way, as he is an adult."*

"I guess now that I stop to think about it, I'm proud of being so caring about someone else who is not aware of purposefully giving me anything in return."

There is no doubt, there has never been any doubt, that we love and idolize our child, and couldn't imagine how we could ever continue to live happily if something happened to her. Yet at the same time, we are still learning what it is to be a mother. We might not now experience such negative periods as we did a few months ago, though we still find ourselves weighing in our minds the rewards versus what we've given up. More often now, they come up at least equal.

Suggested Reading:

Passages: Predictable Crises of Adult Life, by Gail Sheehy

CHAPTER
NINE

MONTHS
9 & 10

Three-quarters of the way through the baby's first year, we frequently find ourselves in the role of intermediary between the child and the world. As the baby moves around more efficiently, we are called upon to anticipate and remove dangers. And, as the child's best friend, we facilitate individual play or early socializing with other children. We often find this period of the baby's life to be exciting, but also quite demanding. There is little time to relax or socialize or daydream when the baby is awake.

Mobility

The baby's slow-paced, tentative crawl has matured into a well-developed method of locomotion. Babies at this stage can most likely cover territory on all fours almost as fast as we can on two feet. They are beginning to "get into everything." We are scurrying to buy special cabinet latches and electrical outlet covers. Plants have to be hung or somehow disposed of. Books must be packed into the shelves or else raised out of the child's reach. The coffee table has to be cleared of ashtrays and magazines if we don't want to be constantly guarding them or picking them up off the floor. Toys are scattered everywhere.

We quickly become inventors of all sorts of ingenious tricks to safeguard the environment. Lamps that can be jerked off the table by a pull on the cord may be suspended with picture-hanging wire from the ceiling while still touching the table. Screws are placed in window frames so the windows will only open a few inches. Trash baskets are to found on top of shelves or desks or in latched cabinets. Gates are strung across stairs or rooms that can't be child-proofed. Sharp edges are padded.

All of this is in respomse to the baby's mobility and to our interest in safety. Earlier, when we had total control of our baby's environment—they would stay where we put them—we could at least be sure, if we walked out of the room, that they wouldn't hurt themselves in any major way. That kind of assurance is never to be taken for granted anymore. This is the beginning of concerns over physical dangers to our children that will never cease. She might swallow something that will stick in her throat. In a year, we will be concerned that he will run out into the street.

This new anxiety about her safety is one thing we feel at this point, as we child-proof the house. But we also may feel twinges of loss when we look around and see that the place is barren from the floor up to about three feet. Treasures we've collected over the years, plants we've nurtured, arrangements of furniture and lamps and books that were always comfortable and attractive have been moved and replaced with a never-ending jumble of safe toys. We might regret or even resent the transition from a house for adults to a kid's house. It seems to signify how much the baby has altered our lives. Our space has been invaded and taken over.

Once again, we do what is necessary for the child's well-being, often without question, but it should at least be noted if we feel regretful. To deny the feeling or to believe that it should have no validity is to disrespect ourselves.

At the same time, however, we are totally charmed by the baby, who has never been cuter or more rewarding. The child's expressions, actions, attractions, and displeasures daily indicate more and more about the personality that is unfolding. There really never has been a more delightful, bright, lovable child in the whole world, we're convinced.

Play

The baby has been "playing" for months. It could be argued that simply waving their arms and changing facial expressions, or moving the bowels is "play," for infants. But around nine or ten months there seems to be a jump in our children's inquisitiveness about objects and people. We are able to recognize more of what they are doing as "play" as we understand it. And more and more, we are drawn in as her special playmate.

In this, as in other aspects of our mothering, researchers have found that we instinctively perform as the child needs us to. One of our roles in play, at this age and beyond, is that of a "facilitator." As Rudolph Schaffer explains in *Mothering:*

"A large part of a mother's time is devoted to such quietly facilitative and scene-setting activities as holding a toy that seems to require three hands to manipulate, retrieving things that have been pushed out of range, clearing away those things that are not at present being used in order to provide the child with a sharper focus for this main activity, putting things next to each other that she knows the child will enjoy combining (such as nesting beakers), turning toys so that they become more easily grasped, demonstrating their less obvious properties, and all along molding her body in such a way as to provide maximal physical support and access to the play material."[1]

There is this kind of attentiveness when the child is close to us. At other times, we are constantly monitoring the child's focus of interest. "Mothers rarely follow every one of the infant's looks," Schaffer writes, "but they normally remain sufficiently attuned to be continuously aware of direction of his interest, and are thus in a position to predict what he wil do next (such as reach for the object). What is more, establishing mutual attention is often only the first step in a whole series: mothers may not only look where the infant is looking, but also may then comment on what he sees, label it, and in other ways verbally elaborate upon it. Thus mother and infant come to share experiences—a sharing generally instigated by the infant's spontaneous interest in his surroundings but established by the mother's allowing herself to be paced by the baby."[2]

The combination of these two activities on our part means that we are closely attuned to the child's environment and are acting as mediator who stimulates, encourages, facilitates, and who is aware of the child's reactions. In all of this our role is a passive one.

The other role we assume is the more active one of actual playmate—who crawls around the room, plays peek-a-boo and bouncing games, who rolls balls and stacks blocks, who laughs at the same things that amuse the child and generally acts like a ten-month-old for awhile. More and more frequently the baby demands that kind of active playmate role from us, since it is far more fun to interact with someone in play than just to play alone. Often babies will cry now simply for us to play with them, to share their enjoyment of toys and physical romping around. Though their attention span for any one given activity is very short, the overall length of time they choose to play now occupies most of their waking hours.

At this age, when babies have our undivided attention as a playmate, there is a tendency to wait for us to initiate the games or to demonstrate the entertaining qualities of toys. They grow bored quickly with making up the activities themselves: most likely they are incapable of being the instigator very much of the time. They wait for us to show them. This may be different from what we had expected of kids. We tend to remember our after-school imaginative games or the hours spent fooling around with some new gadget to see how it worked. Ten-month-olds do not spend much time alone given a choice, nor do they automatically possess the skills necessary to be self-entertaining for very long. We are called to their aid. And their fussiness is a stringent reminder.

Sometimes we can patiently perform as we are wanted to, playing with the child for stretches of half an hour or longer, and we probably enjoy the time ourselves. The child's enthusiastic glee is contagious. But even on the best of days the baby has the ability to play far beyond our point of interest. We get up to do something else and there are screams of protest.

"It's funny, because on the one hand, I am really fascinated with her. I love to watch her, listen to her babble, but I don't like to have to entertain her for long periods of time."

"She always played extremely well by herself. And I am not that interested in actively playing with her all the time. Because of this, I think it would probably be good if she could be with people who stimulated her, and at this point, that would be other children."

Many new mothers at this point, if not before, try to find a playmate or two of the child's age for a couple of mornings or afternoons a week. While ten-month-olds do not actually play *together* (cooperative play doesn't begin until about two and a half or three), they are obviously stimulated by and fascinated with each other. It's a pleasure to be relieved of the entertainment role and also interesting and fun to watch the children interact. They crawl around discovering new toys or familiar old ones that suddenly seem more enthralling than they have in weeks. They bang toys and watch for responses in the other child. They pull curiously at the feet and ears and hair of each other—which calls for intervention. Generally, they watch and learn from the other small people and are completely intrigued.

For a while we've probably been aware of how much our children are attracted to other children; they seem to recognize in them a link to themselves, or maybe it's just that they find other children more amusing than slow-moving, serious adults. This awareness is further strengthened by seeing the children together. Whereas we have to work at playing with a child, the children take over themselves, require very little instigation from us, and seem to have a better time than with us alone.

Our children are social beings who enjoy relating to people like themselves, just as we do. Though we are unique and irreplaceable to them, we are not always the best playmates, either from our or from their point of view. It is gratifying to introduce them into the social world and see them enjoy it so much, to know that even from this early age friendships can be important to them. We feel that we are doing the right thing in encouraging sociability and in allowing our children to play at their own pace, meeting their own needs.

There are, of course, frequent conflicts when kids are together. The same toy invariably attracts two children at once, who struggle and cry over it. One child seems to be more aggressive and assertive, hitting or pulling to get his own way. Another child is quiet and shy, preferring to sit on her mother's lap rather than join in. Another child may howl if anyone approaches his little mound of toys. Still another might be unpredictably docile one moment and a conniver the next.

Children's personalities seem to show up in relief against the backdrop of interaction with other kids. We might never have realized how shy or tolerant or assertive our child was until we see her with others. We begin to have questions about childhood sociability. When is it appropriate to ask a child to share? Is it right to punish a young child who hits? Should we intervene in every conflict over toys or allow the children to work it out themselves?

Certainly, with our children at ten months of age, many of these questions answer themselves. We do what feels best to us at the time, without pushing the child in one direction or another, and attempt to be equitable in solving confrontations. But this is the beginning of the sorts of social questions that will persist for a long time. The children know only what they want. Slowly, we have to help them to understand that other people are involved and their needs must be considered also. This involves a long, gradual teaching process that seems to become more subtle and intricate as time goes on.

> *"When to teach sharing or something about in-dependence? 'Take it as it comes' is my rule. Just recently my boy has begun expressing his sense of power over people and things, and he is very much in-to 'my' and 'mine.' So I have begun teaching him about sharing—which he seems to understand sometimes and not at other times. This is fine with me and I don't feel I need to pressure him.*
>
> *"In regards to independence—I think we decided he needed to feel more independent from us when we ourselves felt pressured by his dependence when he was about a year old. Now it seems like we have a comfortable balance. I don't seem to need to push him away when he needs to depend on me."*

"It seems that my daughter has absolutely no idea of the concept of sharing if it is something she really wants. Yet, she usually lets other children play freely with her toys. My idea is that if she has something in her hand I will not let another child grab it away from her, and that goes vice versa too.

"Although she is very sweet she can hold her own, so I am trying not to interfere too much. However, I find that I am deciding who she will and will not play with, as I am concerned about her picking up aggresive habits from other children."

If we feel that our children are too quiet or too dominating, we have to look carefully at the situation they are in. Maybe something in that particular group is eliciting such behavior. And we need also to examine our own values about personalities. As we might have noted earlier, perhaps the child's temperament is different from ours. That doesn't necessarily mean that the child is *too* much one way or another. It may be that putting a value judgement on the child's behavior is an added burden to both of us.

Sometimes other mothers make us feel worse about this, saying, "Terry certainly does know how to get her way, doesn't she?" Or, "Susie's so quiet. Is she tired?" Further, we sometimes act out of embarrassment, as if our children are a direct extension of ourselves. If our child takes another child's toy, even though we understand his attraction to it, we may rush to the other child's defense just to please the other observing mother. We may not feel that our child has been that bad, but we don't know what the other mother is thinking, and we'd prefer, at least, to pretend that our child can begin to show some social graces.

Chances are that no social behavior at this point in the child's life is bad or inappropriate—but merely natural. Ten-month-olds are too young for us to expect that they consider anyone's feelings but their own. Their enthusiasms, whims, and aggressions are all uncomplicated expressions of their feelings, and we should take them as such.

This does not deny the fact that we are now confronted with a fresh set of questions and challenges. For we are being asked to look closely at the child's social behavior and development. This is a more complex task than fostering physical development. We have to look at our own values, consider other people's reactions, and figure out ways to guide the child along a path to successful, enjoyable social interaction over the course of the next several years.

In short, we are rapidly becoming aware that the first few months of motherhood—which seemed so strenuous—were in some ways simpler than what we are dealing with now. We are starting to realize that motherhood is a tremendously complex, emotionally demanding experience that challenges and develops our understanding and expertise about life in many ways.

MONTHS 11 & 12

Nearly a year has gone by, we realize, a year of tremendous changes in ourselves and in our child. Somehow we had always thought of the first birthday as a landmark in the child's independence and in our regaining more of our personal lives. And so, as the landmark approaches we begin to evaluate where we are and where we're going.

Lately, too, the baby might have been irritable and demanding as before other developmental steps. We know enough now to understand that this fussiness is probably preceeding walking. We look forward to that momentous event, but have little patience for the child's frustration.

As we have been mothers for almost a full year, it is a good time to examine how we've progressed and to look at our feelings about parenthood. As has been true before, simply recognizing the feelings and trying to sort out their origins will make us feel more confident and more normal.

The Individual, and Our Reactions

There is no doubt that the child has a mind of its own now. If we leave the room and she doesn't like our timing, there are howls. If we're cooking dinner when she wants to play, our legs are tugged at and an effort is made to push us away from the stove. The child might resist getting dressed, eating, sleeping, or getting in the stroller or backpack. In short, this is not the easiest person to live with any more. When awake, she demands our undivided attention most of the time, and is definitely beginning to sleep less.

We're acquainted with this behavior somewhat. There were rocky times around separation anxiety and the beginning of crawling. But the eleven-month-old can anticipate our actions or plans often, knows which protests are the most effective, and so is not as easily distracted as before.

We speculate that maybe we are the cause of the child's irritability, and at times feel drained. Yet as soon as the troublemaker is asleep in bed at night, we are overwhelmed by our love and regret our impatience.

"If she doesn't settle down I scold her and relatively soon in the game put her in her crib. It seems that separating her from us is just what she needs, and it does not seem to be a punishment for her. The next thing you know she is babbling and singing to her multitude of stuffed animals in her crib. I have a theory that parents should do this at a very ear-

ly age. To reinforce good behavior, they shouldn't spank but just teach that if children want to be with the parents they have to be pleasant."

Values

As we recognize that at this stage children are separate individuals with their own needs, preoccupations, and personalities, we inevitably also face ourselves—as though looking in a mirror. The child is able now as never before to express her preferences, displeasures, and temperamental idiosyncracies; and we find ourselves saying, "Yes, she is just like me in that," or "*Where* did that obnoxious trait of his come from?" It is at about this time that we start to realize the impact of our nurturance—which contributes to the child's personality as much as any natural traits she or he might have been born with.

For instance, we might have decided that we want our children to have one particular type of diet as opposed to another. We feel that this will make them healthier, and instill in their taste buds a preference for the foods we think are the best. We might have determined that they will watch little or no TV. We think their playmates should be wholesome children whose mothers share, for the most part, our basic philosophy of child-raising. These things we can pretty much control.

Then there is the question of knowing very well what values we'd like our children to have but not knowing when or how it is best to try to instill them. Mothers would like their children to be honest, caring, helpful, curious, patient, and happy, to name a few. But beyond providing an example of that in ourselves, are there other ways to pass those traits along? And when can we expect that our children will be caring enough about animals not to pull their ears, or patient enough not to scream about a short ride in the car?

And then there is the question of those values that we are passing along while hardly being aware of it. They are values about lifestyle, language, sociability, family, roles, attitudes, and concern or lack of concern about the rest of the world. We live those things, and our children learn from them. Much of this area is nearly hidden from us until we see it emerge in the child. Then we are either pleased with ourselves and our system of values or disturbed. Either way, our children force us to look at ourselves more closely.

"I now realize that it is inevitable that I'll be passing on to my son both the good things and the negative traits I have, and that's okay.

"I do not control my anger, nor do I exceed with it. I do not control my flow of curses when a situation brings them out, although he makes me feel more self-conscious than I used to feel. And I do not hide my tears. In short, I give him all that I am and hope that the good parts will balance out the others as he is growing up. My husband and I have agreed to disagree on some of our differences about how to bring him up. And I hope that this awareness will keep him out of confusion—the best we can hope for."

"I am glad to have him playing with the many different kinds and races of children we have in our neighborhood. I don't want him to ever have to think other people are odd or frightening just because he is unfamiliar with them. I went through that, having been around only white, Anglo-Saxon, Protestant people as a child, and later I had to deal with the prejudices that had unknowingly been passed down to me."

"My husband and I both feel much more strongly our commitment to the anti-nuclear movement because of our child. I don't want her living forty years of her

*life in an underground cave because we contaminated
the surface of the earth. In general, my political values
have been strengthened. Spiritually, I am not a
religious person, yet I now feel the need to have some
kind of formal spiritual training passed on. I never had
any religious training as a child, and I guess I feel a
lack."*

Part of the joy of child-raising is watching a kind of beautiful unfolding that, we can see, has been partly influenced by us and our careful, painstaking efforts, and partly is simply the natural unfolding of a personality that is inherently, elementally its own.

And that is the other half of this whole realm of values. What do we see in our children and how does that match up to our expectations? At this age, we know enough about our children to know some of their basic personality traits. We have to begin to recognize these as innate characteristics and to respect them.

For many of us this does not come naturally at first—particularly if the child is very different from us in certain ways. Or conversely, the child might have a trait of ours that we've secretly tried to hide because we've disliked it in ourselves.

One woman, talking about the due date of her baby, said, "Oh, I hope it's a Pisces instead of an Aquarian. I like practical, down-to-earth people. I couldn't stand to have a dreamer around." In a humorous way, this illustrates the expectations we all carry around with us about our children. We hope to have children with whom we will have no conflicts. And yet, children are who they are, and gradually we have to realize and accept that. Otherwise we do them the harmful disservice of not approving of their very essences.

*"We had expected a quiet, placid baby, since we
are both peaceful in a way. And then here comes this
rambunctious boy who requires so much of our energy
and attention. We have come to appreciate that spirit*

*in him of adventurousness and extroverted liveliness
so different from ourselves. But we still wonder where
it came from, and still hope that he'll calm down just a
little bit some day."*

Most mothers *do* respect what their children are, though they may not totally accept all their children's characteristics at first. Gradually, as they see the differences between themselves and their children, they begin to appreciate these differences as complements to themselves. After all, if we are "practical, and down-to-earth," a "dreamer" could expose buried sides of ourselves that need airing now and then. The mutual influence can be stimulating and refreshing for parents and children alike. That is part of the miracle and beauty of our individual uniqueness. We have so much more to offer each other that way.

Sometimes, to be sure, it's difficult to know when we're disciplining an overly rowdy child or squelching the child's "spirit." It's hard to separate encouragement from pushing; difficult to know for certain what can be expected of a twelve-month-old or a two- or five-year-old. As is true of much of motherhood, a great deal is built on instinct and what we know of our particular children whom we love and grow to like as people.

Modern Parents

Increasingly, we become aware, as our children grow that there are special pleasures and problems with each stage. And at every stage we ask if we're doing things right. Such doubts are normal and predictable, because this entire experience is new. Just when we feel that we have it all figured out, our children challenge us in some new way. We are knocked off balance again until we readjust. This is simply the normal life of a first-time parent.

However, there are certain factors in raising children in this half of the twentieth century that contribute to parental feelings of insecurity and fallibility. This theme is elaborated in *Parents in Modern America* by E. E. LeMasters, a pioneer in the study of transitions to parenthood.[1] He enumerates how sociological changes in the last thirty years have made parenthood an even more difficult task than before.

One of the major factors he cites is that there are higher standards now for parents than in our grandparents' or parents' day. There is considerable social pressure put on parents to produce children who are better than the parents are. In this society of upward mobility and progress, every generation should supposedly, top the previous one. According to one's system of values that might mean that our children should be more financially successful, or more personable, or more educated, or more sophisticated—but anyway, better.

Further, parents are not judged by their peers—other parents—but by professionals; psychologists, educators, and child specialists, who imply that if something is wrong with the child, it is automatically assumed to be the parents' fault. This has spawned what LeMasters calls the "cult of the child:" the child is perfect and everything must be sacrificed for the child. These are impossibly high standards and of questionable value. Are professionals, for example, actually better judges of what should be done with children than the parents who have spent so much more time with them and who love them? Should everything be sacrificed for children or do they learn to recognize the needs of others as well as their own through social interaction and cooperation?

A second important point is that the rate of social change is so great that there are conflicting norms within our present-day society. What was standard, acceptable behavior for children when we were growing up is questioned today. For instance, though our parents were probably not domineering, we nevertheless grew up with a healthy respect for our parents' wishes and demands. For the most part, we obeyed curfews and dating restrictions. We were taught to respect our elders and their traditions. Now, in this age of healthy skepticism, many parents doubt that they should require such unquestioning reverence or obedience from their children. We feel it is perhaps wiser to instill in them a spirit of rebellion. And yet, that places us directly in their line of fire. LeMasters says, parental authority has been eroded over a period of decades, without any reduction in parental responsibility.

Another effect of accelerating social change is that we don't know what sort of world we're preparing our children for. Whole social orders have changed so dramatically in the last fifteen years that it is valid to assume that things could be very different for our children fifteen years from now. But how will we prepare them for what we know nothing about?

Third, the structure of the family has been and is evolving, and the strains inevitable in the evolution of such a basic social unit are apparent within the family members themselves. Families are much smaller now than they were in our parent's generation. Such a concentration among a few people means that the relationships are all very intense and not diffused as they can be in larger families.

Families move a lot. Fifty percent of the United States population moves every five years according to the 1970 census. That means families are continually thrown back on themselves, rather than receiving continuing support from community and friends. Roles within the family, once so defined and explicit, are changing; and each family has to sort out for itself what works best for each member and for the unit. Frequently, these roles have to be renegotiated as the family ages.

All of these factors can fuel doubts about our ability to be good parents. In an era when everything seems to be shifting, it is not surprising that such an inherently complex task as parenting would be even more complex. There are no solid rules: it is strictly learn as we go, depend on our own sense of values and judgments, and hope that we do a good enough job.

And so as the first year draws to a close, we find ourselves in some ways much more confident. We're not as upset by our child's fussiness, because we know it is just a phase he is passing through and we've learned some methods to help keep ourselves sane in the process. We are pleased to know that the first flushes of love we felt for the child have grown and deepened so that we are terribly thankful for the gift of love we've been shown and that we return to the child.

But we also wonder about the future, and about the complexities of the situations and feelings we're suddenly facing with the child. There are always questions in our minds about whether we are doing all that we can to help our child grow into the inspiring young adult we'd like her to be. Though somehow we feel now that we'll manage.

Suggested Reading:

Growing Up Free: Raising Your Child in the 80's, by Letty Cottin Pogrebin

Your Child's Self-Esteem, by Dorothy Corkille Briggs

The Magic Years, by Selma Fraiberg

Parents in Modern America, by E. E. LeMasters

EPILOGUE

Much has been accomplished in this year, despite our doubts and occasional feelings of inadequacy. We have successfully raised a child from a state of total helplessness and dependency to be a mobile, complex individual. Reflecting on these dramatic changes, we may neglect to acknowledge the less observable, but nonetheless profound, changes that have occurred in us. The child has raised us to a new understanding of life and of ourselves.

From the first ecstatic, bewildering days with the new baby, throughout the months of waiting for more responses from the child, to the whirlwind of demands and excitements thrust upon us in these last few months, we have been aware of often feeling off-balance. Now we understand that those feelings were signs of the tremendous changes and adjustments we were making in the transition to motherhood. Only twenty-four percent of mothers surveyed in one study felt that they had overcome the "crisis" of transition to motherhood by the time their children were twelve months old.[1] For many of us, it seems, the feelings of insecurity remain long after the end of the first year. This is not due to our inabilities, but rather to the vast scope of the changes that must occur in us. The emotional adjustments that take place are profound—and may take years.

We must reorient our outward lives regarding career options—making difficult decisions about whether to postpone a career and the type of fulfillment it gives us, or to assume that being with our young children is the highest priority for us right now. We must restrict our entertainment, social, and individual pursuits. We must examine and often alter the nature of our relationships to husbands and parents, and other significant people in our lives. We must learn how to comfortably and efficiently care for a child while developing with the child a unique bond that is probably the most intimate and compelling link that exists with another human being.

Reorientation must occur inwardly, too, as we begin to see and accept an entirely new side of our selves, as our self-image shifts to accommodate the role and feelings of a mother. This inner adjustment is, at times, the most challenging and troublesome because we must actually relinquish part of our old style and the satisfactions it had given us, in order to admit an evolving self that can at first seem less attractive or gratifying. Such a basic identity change is physically and emotionally draining. Regret may accompany the necessity to change, and yet, we may also feel we shouldn't have such feelings about motherhood. We often take great pains to ignore or repress the very emotions that are leading us on to the next stage in our development as mothers.

This next stage involves acceptance of ourselves as mothers

and understanding the nature of motherhood. It might be reached at the end of the first year, or not for many more months. Such major life transitions, requiring growth and maturation, and take extended periods of time.

Most women see motherhood as a challenging, ultimately maturing experience, so that despite the long-term disorientation that can be involved, we do end up in a different, solid place that affords us grander views. We begin to understand, as never before, parental love and concern as a fundamental part of life. We have experienced, because of our children, vast new dimensions of love, guilt, anger, compassion, and giving. We have been forced to see beyond ourselves and our own needs. All of this is revealing and dramatic. We tend to feel more aware and insightful about life. We feel ourselves as a respectable link in a generational chain extending down through history.

Of course we are especially grateful for the child who has been entrusted to us. The year has been a long one, perhaps the longest we can remember since being children ourselves. Yet, we know we would never have traded the experience or elected not to have done it. The child has enriched and expanded life for us in so many meaningful ways that the depth of love we feel for the child can still bring spontaneous thankful tears to our eyes when we think about it.

We have had indications in the last few months that the task of child-raising does not get much easier. In some ways, what will be required of us will be more sophisticated and challenging, but because of our experiences so far, we feel more confident and able to do what will be necessary. We realize now that being a mother means continual readjustment in conjunction with the needs of the child. But we also know that our satisfaction with our child and our love for her will continue to grow too, and that because of all this, we will be wiser, happier women as the years go by.

FOOTNOTES

Chapter One

[1]Elise Fitzpatrick, Sharon Reeder, Luigi Mastrioanni, Jr., *Maternity Nursing,* p. 303.

[2]Nicholson J. Eastman and Louis M. Hellman, *Williams Obstetrics,* p. 476.

[3]Ibid.

[4]Reva Rubin, "Puerperal Change." *Nursing Outlook* 9,(December 1961):753.

[5]Ibid.

[6]Ibiḑ.

[7]Ibid.

[8]Ibid., 754

[9]Ibid.

[10]Ibid.

[11]Marshall H. Klaus et al., "Human Maternal Behavior at the First Contact with Her Young." *Pediatrics* 46,(August 1970):187-191.

[12]Lee Salk, "The Critical Nature of the Postpartum Period in the Human Establishment of the Mother-Infant Bond: A Controlled Study." *Diseases of the Nervous System* 31,(Supp. 1970):110.

[13]K. Robson, The Role of Eye-to-Eye Contact in Maternal-Infant Attachment." *Journal of Child Psychology and Psychiatry* 8,No. 1(May, 1967):13-23.

[14]Marshall H. Klaus et al., "Maternal Attachment—Importance of the First Post-Partum Days." *New England Journal of Medicine* 286,(March 2, 1972):460-63.

[15]Karen Pryor, *Nursing Your Baby,* p. 185.

[16]Bibring, Grete L. et al., "A Study of the Psychological Processes in Pregnancy and of the Earliest Mother-Child Relationship." *The Psychoanalytic Study of the Child* 16,(1961):9-72.

Chapter Two

[1]Betsy Lozoff et al., "The Mother-Newborn Relationship: Limits of Adaptability." *The Journal of Pediatrics* 91(July 1977):2.

[2]Ibid., p. 3.

[3]Ibid.

[4]Ibid.

[5]D.M. Levy, *Behavioral Analysis* (Springfield, Ill.: Thomas, 1958).

[6]A.H. Parmelee et al., "Infants' Sleep Patterns from Birth to 16 Weeks of Age." *Journal of Pediatrics*65,(1964):576-82.

[7]Ibid.

Chapter Three

[1]Theodore Lidz, "The Effects of Children on Marriage." In *The Marriage Relationship,* Salo Rosenbaum and Ian Alger, eds., p. 122.

[2]Erik H. Erikson, "Identity and the Life Cycle." In *Psychological Issues,* p. 55.

[3]Joseph Meyerowitz and Harold Feldman, "Transition to Parenthood." *Psychiatric Research Report* 20,(1966): 78-84.

[4]Ibid.

[5]Everett D. Dyer, "Parenthood as Crisis: A Re-Study." *Marriage and Family Living* 25,(May 1963): 196-201.

[6]Daniel F. Hobbs, Jr. and Sue Peck Coles, "Transition to Parenthood: A Decade Replication." *Journal of Marriage and the Family,* 38,(November 1976):723-31.

[7]Meyerowitz and Feldman, "Transition to Parenthood."

[8]Lidz, *"The Effects of Children on Marriage,"* p. 125.

[9]Meyerowitz and Feldman, "Transition to Parenthood."

[10]William H. Masters and Virginia E. Johnson, *Human Sexual Response, pp. 150-52, 161-63.*

[11]*Hobbes and Coles, "Transition to Parenthood."*

[12]*Robert Fein, "Men's Experiences Before and After the Birth of a First Child: Dependence, Marital Sharing, and Anxiety." Dissertation Abstracts,* 35, (March, April 1975):5082B.

Chapter Four

[1]Therese Benedek, "Parenthood During the Life Cycle," *Parenthood: Its Psychology and Psychopathology,* E. James Anthony and Therese Benedek, eds. (Boston: Little, Brown & Co., 1970), p. 201.

[2]Therese Benedek, "Parenthood as a Developmental Phase," *Journal of the American Psychoanalytic Association* 7,(July 1959):395.

[3]Ibid., p. 396.

Chapter Five

[1]Reva Rubin, "Maternity Care in Our Society," *Nursing Outlook* 11,(July 1963):521.

[2]Nicholson J. Eastman and Louis M. Hellman, *Williams Obstetrics,* p. 479

[3]Grete L. Bibring et al., "A Study of the Psychological Processes in Pregnancy and of the Earliest Mother-Child Relationship," *The Psychoanalytic Study of the Child* 16(1961):9-72.

[4]Beauty D. Crummette, "Transitions in Motherhood," *Maternal-Child Nursing Journal* 4,No. 2(Summer 1975):68-9.

[5]K.E. Gordon et al., "Factors in Postpartum Emotional Adjustment," *Obstetrics and Gynecology* 25,(February 1965):158-66.

[6]Everett D. Dyer, "Parenthood as Crisis: A Re-Study," *Marriage and Family Living,* 25,(May 1963):196-201.

[7]Daniel F. Hobbs, Jr. and Sue Peck Cole, "Transition to Parenthood: A Decade Replication," *Journal of Marriage and the Family* 38,(November 1976):723-31.

[8]Joseph Meyerowitz and Harold Feldman, "Transition to Parenthood," *Psychiatric Research Report* 20,(January 1966):78-84.

[9]Bibring, "A Study of the Psychological Processes in Pregnancy," p. 26.

[10]Dyer.

[11]Therese Benedek, "On the Psychic Economy of Developmental Processes," *Archives of General Psychiatry,* 17,(September 1967):271.

[12]William Bridges, *The Seasons of Our Lives.*

Chapter Six

[1]K. Robson, "The Role of Eye-to-Eye Contact in Maternal-Infant Attachment," *Journal of Child Psychology and Psychiatry*, 8,(1967):13-23.

[2]Rudolf Schaffer, *Mothering*, p. 65.

[3]Judy Dunn, *Distress and Comfort*, p. 18.

[4]Lee Salk and Rita Kramer, *How to Raise a Human Being*, p. 56.

[5]Shirley Radl, *Mother's Day Is Over*, p. 7.

[6]Elaine Heffner, *Mothering: The Emotional Experience of Motherhood after Freud and Feminism* p. 28.

[7]Ibid., p. 30.

[8]Ibid., p. 30-31.

[9]Ibid., p. 34.

[10]Ibid., p. 43.

[11]Everett D. Dyer, "Parenthood as Crisis: A Re-Study," *Marriage and Family Living* 25,(May 1963):196-201.

[12]Alice S. Rossi, "Transition to Parenthood," *Journal of Marriage and the Family*, 30,(February 1968):34.

[13]Arlene Rossen Cardozo, *Woman at Home*.

Chapter Seven

[1]Jerome Kagan, *The Growth of the Child: Reflections on Human Development*.

[2]Mary C. Howell, "Employed Mothers and Their Families," *Pediatrics* 52,(August 1973):252.

[3]Ibid., p. 258.

[4]Jean Curtis, *Working Mothers*, p. 58.

[5]Ibid., p. 40.

Chapter Eight

[1]Erik H. Erikson, "Identity and the Life Cycle." In *Psychological Issues*, p. 95.

[2]Ibid., p. 97.

[3]Ibid.

[4]Ibid., p. 98.

Chapter Nine

[1]Rudolph Schaffer, *Mothering*, p. 73.

[2]Ibid., pp. 70-1.

Chapter Ten

[1]E.E. LeMasters, *Parents in Modern America, (Homewood, Ill.: The Dorsey Press, 1977).*

Epilogue

[1]Everett Dyer, "Parenthood as Crisis: A Re-Study," *Marriage and Family Living,* 25,(1963):197.

BIBLIOGRAPHY

Abrahamsen, David. *The Emotional Care of Your Child.* New York: Pocket Books, 1969.

Anthony, E. James, and Benedek, Therese, eds. *Parenthood—Its Psychology and Psychopathology.* Boston: Little, Brown & Co., 1970.

Barber, Virginia, and Skaggs, Merrill Maguire. *The Mother Person.* New York: Bobbs-Merrill, 1975.

Boston Women's Health Book Collective. *Ourselves and Our Children.* New York: Random House, 1978.

Boston Women's Health Book Collective. *Our Bodies, Ourselves.* New York, Simon & Schuster, 1973.

Brazelton, T. Berry. *Infants and Mothers.* New York, Delacorte, 1969.

Bridges, William. *The Seasons of Our Lives,* Rolling Hills Estates, Ca., The Wayfarer Press, 1977.

Briggs, Dorothy Corkille. *Your Child's Self-Esteem.* Garden City, N.Y., Doubleday & Co., 1975.

Cardozo, Arlene Rossen. *Woman at Home.* Garden City, N.Y., Doubleday & Co., 1976.

Clark, Ann L. *Culture, Childbearing, Health Professionals.* Philadelphia: F.A. Davis Co., 1978.

Curtis, Jean. *Working Mothers.* Garden City, N.Y., Doubleday & Co., 1976.

Deutsch, Helene. *Psychology of Women.* Vol. 2. New York, Grune & Stratton, 1945.

Deutscher, Max. "First Pregnancy and Family Formation." In *Psychoanalytic Contributions to Community Psychology.* Donald Milman and George Goldman, eds. Springfield, Ill.: Charles C. Thomas, 1971.

Dodson, Fitzhugh. *How to Father.* Los Angeles: Nash, 1974.

Dunn, Judy. *Distress and Comfort.* Developing Child Series. Cambridge, Mass.: Harvard University Press, 1977.

Eastman, Nicholson J., and Hellman, Louis M. *Williams Obstetrics.* New York: Appleton, Century, Crofts, 1961.

Erikson, Erik H. "Identity and the Life Cycle." In *Psychological Issues.* New York: International Universities Press, 1959.

————. *Childhood and Society.* New York: W.W. Norton & Co., 1950.

Elise Fitzpatrick, Sharon Reeder, Luigi Mastroianni, Jr. *Maternity Nursing.* Philadelphia: J.B. Lippincott Co., 1971.

Fraiberg, Selma. *Every Child's Birthright: In Defense of Mothering.* New York: Basic Books, 1977.

Garvey, Catherine. *Play.* Developing Child Series. Cambridge Mass.: Harvard University Press, 1977.

Heffner, Elaine. *Mothering: The Emotional Experience of Motherhood After Freud and Feminism.* Garden City, N.Y.: Doubleday & Co., 1978.

Howell, Mary C. *Helping Ourselves: Families and the Human Network.* Boston: Beacon Press, 1975.

Kagan, Jerome. *The Growth of the Child: Reflections on Human Development.* New York: Norton, 1978.

Kelly, Marguerite, and Parsons, Elia. *Mother's Almanac.* Garden City, N.Y.: Doubleday, 1975.

Kohl, Herbert. *Growing with Your Children.* Boston: Little, Brown & Co., 1978.

Lazarre, Jane. *The Mother Knot.* New York: McGraw-Hill, 1976.

LeMasters, E.E. *Parents in Modern America.* Homewood, Ill.: The Dorsey Press, 1977.

Lidz, Theodore. "The Effects of Children on Marriage." In *The Marriage Relationship.* Salo Rosenbaum and Ian Alger, eds. New York: Basic Books, 1968.

Lipkin, Gladys B. *Psychosocial Aspects of Maternal-Child Nursing.* St. Louis: C.V. Mosby Co., 1974.

Mcfarlane, Aidan. *The Psychology of Childbirth.* Developing Child Series. Cambridge, Mass: Harvard University Press, 1977.

McBride, Angela Barron. *The Growth and Development of Mothers.* New York: Harper & Row, 1973.

Morgan, Robin, ed. "The Dynamics of Marriage and Motherhood." In *Sisterhood Is Powerful.* New York: Random House, 1970.

Peck, Ellen. *The Baby Trap.* New York: Bernard Geis Associates, 1971.

Princeton Center for Infancy and Early Childhood. *The First Twelve Months of Life.* New York: Bantam Books, 1978.

Pryor, Karen. *Nursing Your Baby.* New York: Pocket Books, 1973.

Radl, Shirley L. *Mother's Day Is Over.* New York: Charterhouse, 1973.

Rakowitz, Elly, and Rubin, Gloria S. *Living with Your New Baby: A Post-partum Guide for Mothers and Fathers.* New York: Franklin Watts, 1978.

Rich, Adrienne. *Of Woman Born: Motherhood as Experience and Institution.* New York: W.W. Norton & Co., 1976.

Rozdilsky, Mary Lou, and Banet, Barbara. *What Now? A Handbook for New Parents.* New York: Charles Scribner's Sons, 1975.

Salk, Lee, and Kramer, Rita. *How to Raise a Human Being.* New York: Random House, 1969.

Schaffer, Rudolph. *Mothering.* Developing Child Series. Cambridge, Mass.: Harvard University Press, 1977.

Spock, Benjamin. *Baby and Child Care.* New York: Pocket Books, 1976.

I N D E X